THE LORD'S PRAYER

THE LORD'S PRAYER

A Prayer for All People

BROTHER
DAVID STEINDL-RAST

WITH BRIGITTE KWIZDA-GREDLER

TRANSLATED BY
Patrick Conlin

Paulist Press
New York / Mahwah, NJ

Pllustrations courtesy of Tyrolia-Verlag, Innsbruck. Used with permission.

Scripture quotations are from the New Revised Standard Version Bible: Catholic Edition, copyright © 1989, 1993 National Council of the Churches of Christ in the United States of America. Used by permission. All rights reserved worldwide.

Cover image by logoboom / shutterstock.com
Cover and book design by Lynn Else

Originally published as *Das Vaterunser* by Tyrolia-Verlag, Austria

Library of Congress Cataloging-in-Publication Data
Names: Steindl-Rast, David author | Kwizda-Gredler, Brigitte author | Conlin, Patrick translator
Title: The Lord's prayer: a prayer for all people / Brother David Steindl-Rast with Brigitte Kwizda-Gredler; translated by Patrick Conlin.
Other titles: Vaterunser. English
Description: New York; Mahwah, NJ: Paulist Press, [2025] | Translation of: Das Vaterunser. | Includes bibliographical references. | Text in English. Translation from German. | Summary: "This book is a reflection on the Lord's Prayer so that all people can understand better the Great Mystery of God"—Provided by publisher.
Identifiers: LCCN 2024056200 (print) | LCCN 2024056201 (ebook) | ISBN 9780809157631 paperback | ISBN 9780809189298 ebook
Subjects: LCSH: Lord's prayer—Criticism, interpretation, etc.
Classification: LCC BV230 .S72813 2025 (print) | LCC BV230 (ebook) | DDC 226.9/606—dc23/eng/20250602
LC record available at https://lccn.loc.gov/2024056200
LC ebook record available at https://lccn.loc.gov/2024056201

ISBN 978-0-8091-5763-1 (paperback)
ISBN 978-0-8091-8929-8 (ebook)

Published by Paulist Press
997 Macarthur Boulevard
Mahwah, New Jersey 07430
www.paulistpress.com

Printed and bound in the
United States of America

CONTENTS

CONTENTS

INVITATION TO SILENCE

This book owes its existence to two children. One lives in my memory, the other in my imagination.

I call the imaginary child the "star child of the future"; the one in my memory is me. I kneel next to my grandmother, who has made room for me on her kneeler and prays the Lord's Prayer aloud. Word for word, I memorize this prayer. With the same freshness as the lavender scent of her dress and the ticking of the old wall clock, our prayer times together are still vivid in my memory today. Such memories surface whenever I pray the Lord's Prayer, even now, almost one hundred years later.

At the same time, this prayer personally resonates even deeper. Who taught it to my grandmother? Perhaps one of her grandmothers? Behind them were countless generations of Christians, all the way back to the monks who came from Ireland well over a thousand years ago to the wilderness that would later become Austria, and from them my ancestors learned the Lord's Prayer. Or perhaps their ancestors had learned it even earlier from Christian soldiers in the Roman legions. Salzburg, then called Iuvavum, was a garrison town in the Roman province of Noricum, and many of my ancestors came from this area.

For all Western Christians, not just myself, the whole of Christian Europe and its past resounds when we pray the Lord's Prayer because in past generations everyone in these countries knew this prayer.

The "star child of the future" is also present in my prayers to the Father. That child represents all future generations. Will they also learn to pray the Lord's Prayer? Even today, only a minority of European children still know it. But all of them kneel beside me in the image of the star child as I pray, just as I knelt beside my grandmother. I would like to pass on to this "star child" what I have received. But with which words? Nobody knows the language of the future yet, only that it will be different from ours; this much is clear in such a time of change as ours. This inspired my task, to speak about the Lord's Prayer in such a way that not only Christians, but all people can understand what it is about—because we all have to deal with the Great Mystery that Christians call "God" and "Our Father."

Only those who read this book can decide how far I've succeeded. In any case, I wanted to do so through two methods—reflections and conversations. In the short reflections, I made the Lord's Prayer, which is a community prayer, personally accessible to me. Perhaps this will encourage others to try to do so for themselves. That would make me happy. It wasn't until later that I came back to my reflections and used them as a springboard for conversations by picking out one or two points and talking about them with Brigitte Kwizda-Gredler.

Through her young granddaughter Karlotta, Brigitte has a more tangible relationship with the "star child of the future" than I do. As a medical sociologist, spiritual director, and companion in so-called limit situations such as dementia, dying, and mourning, she is right in the middle of the events of our time, while as a monk I have the perspective of a certain distance. Yet we are profoundly connected by the conscious, lifelong, ever-new encounter with God, the "Great Mystery." Everyone who reads one of our conversations is invited to participate by inwardly disagreeing or agreeing with us; perhaps they even want to continue the conversation outwardly with friends or pick out a point of contemplation that we have not touched on. This could be particularly suitable for reading circles and study groups.

These remarks may sound like a preface but are not meant in this way. The entire Lord's Prayer is actually a single word, "Abba." Its other petitions as well as the considerations and conversations in this book only develop this one word. But before a word, if it is to be a real word, there is not another word, but silence. So instead of a foreword, we invite you here to take a short "foresilence."

Br. David Steindl-Rast

A HIDDEN CHRISTIAN MESSAGE

When we consciously cultivate our personal relationship with the Ultimate Reality, our joy in living grows. This makes gratitude possible and opens the door to joy. What we take for granted leaves us cold. Only what we are grateful for makes our hearts warm and happy. Joy is the kind of happiness that does not depend on what happens to us. Rather, it depends on how grateful we are for what we have been given—whatever it may be. Therefore, we hold the key to the joy of life in our own hands. And gratitude is most intense when it can be directed toward a personal counterpart. The joy it triggers is also greatest then. When we name the source of all good gifts—the Great Mystery, God—and direct our gratitude for the countless gifts of life to this most personal "Thou," then the tree of gratitude, whose fruit is joy, grows immeasurably. And this fruit of joy takes on a very special flavor when we call God "Father."

Calling God "Father" with such emphasis distinguishes the faith tradition that goes back to Jesus from other traditions on the one hand, but at the same time forges a strong link to them.

Because Christians call God "Father," they may call all other people brothers and sisters, because they are also God's children. Indeed, they will not only recognize people, but all creatures as members of God's household and love them accordingly. We urgently need the image of the "earth household" in our time. The American writer Gary Snyder used this term to express his conviction that all living beings belong together and are a gift to one another.

Although I haven't solved a crossword puzzle since my primary school days, I am fascinated by word games and words in general. These include palindromes, which are words that can be read in both directions—from left to right, as we usually read, and also from right to left, as we read Hebrew, for example. The name Anna would be such a word, or a longer "racecar" or even sentences such as "Was it a cat I saw?" Some words take on a new meaning when you read them the other way round, for example: "brag/grab," "dog/god" or the rather profound "live/evil." The longer such words become, the more precious they seem to me, for example, the phrase "repentance = purgatory" or the admonition to lazy pupils "Read, dear!" The saying *Reizend lügt güldne Zier* is particularly pretty, which also makes the same sense when read in both directions.[1]

What does this have to do with the Lord's Prayer? The central content of this prayer was represented in secret very early on in the Christian tradition by the Sator Square. Such magic squares were very popular in antiquity and still are today. For example, see the magic number square depicted on Albrecht Dürer's copperplate engraving *Melencolia* I.

MELENCOLIA I

16 3 2 13
5 10 11 8
9 6 7 12
4 15 14 1

This square of numbers can also be read like a palindrome from left to right and from right to left. In any direction, whether from top to bottom or from left to right, even in the diagonals, the sum is always 34.

In contrast, the Sator Square does not contain numbers, but a palindrome sentence, that is, a sentence that can be read from its beginning or end and means the same thing in both directions. The Sator square contains the Latin sentence *Sator Arepo tenet opera rotas*. In English, this can be translated as "The sower Arepo holds the wheels through his work." The sentence sounds forced and its meaning is also unclear. Since Sator is also a name for the creator of the world in ancient texts (*sator rerum, sator et redemptor*), there is probably a religious meaning contained in the sentence. In this case, Sator refers to the "Cosmic Sower" who holds the *rotas*, the wheels of the universe, in his hands. As Creator, God did not only sow the world, leaving it to its own devices, but God also holds the wheels of the universe carefully in God's hands. *Tenet*, "he/she/it holds," is obviously the central statement in this sentence. The fact that it is placed here in the Sator Square in the shape of a cross makes one think of a Christian origin.

The oldest known Sator Square was discovered in ancient Pompeii, where it can be seen in the Large Palaestra. It must have been created before the eruption of Vesuvius in 79 CE. Later examples can be found wherever Roman soldiers were stationed, from England and Portugal to Mesopotamia. My friend, Dr. Helmut Milz, whose family name still refers to the Roman soldiers, the *milites*, who spread the square abroad, once showed me one. In SS. Peter and Paul Church on the Westerbuchberg, a hill in the town of Übersee not far from Lake Chiemsee in Bavaria, there is a medieval Sator Square hidden under a ceiling that was later raised and vaulted. In the Middle Ages, this square was often used as a magical symbol to ward off rabies, fires, and all other evil. If we allow the strange text to really take effect on us, then even today—far removed from all abracadabra—we can still sense

S	A	T	O	R
A	R	E	P	O
T	E	N	E	T
O	P	E	R	A
R	O	T	A	S

and admire the mysterious power that the letters carry within them. But there is still much more hidden in it.

The meaning of the Sator Square was completely obscure for more than one thousand years. It was not until the early twentieth century that scholars rediscovered that it was originally a very early Christian secret symbol. If you rearrange the twenty-five letters from the Sator square, you get the words Pater Noster, or "Our Father," twice when the letters are arranged in the shape of a cross. All the letters are used up, leaving only two *a*'s and two *o*'s, which represent alpha and omega, the first and last letters of the Greek alphabet. As a symbol, these two letters refer to Christ as the beginning and the end and give the newly created image an even deeper meaning. In the Book of Revelation, the last book in the New Testament, Jesus says, "I am the Alpha and the Omega, the first and the last, the beginning and the end" (Rev 22:13). Only initiates probably knew the deeper meaning of

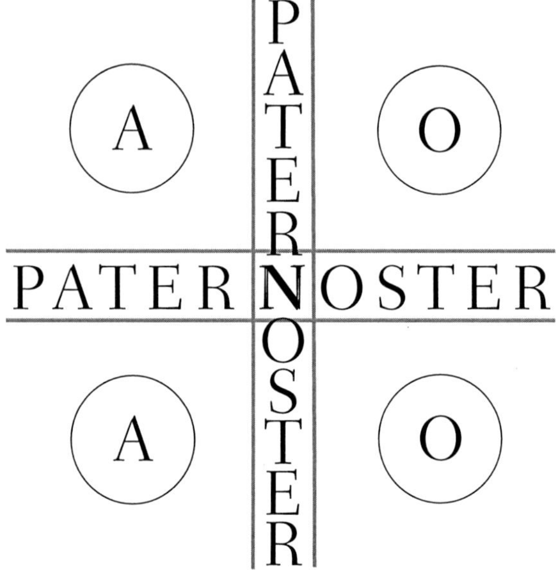

this secret symbol. Apparently, the square was created as an encoding of faith in God as "Our Father."

This belief has its roots in Judaism, and the cross with arms of the same length is also a pre-Christian symbol. As a compass rose, it can signify the entire universe. A cross is also the mark par excellence with which those who cannot write sign documents. In this way, God has inscribed God's name on the universe as the Father of us all. The crossed *tenet* in the magic square, which means "he holds," or "he holds together," therefore refers to the Father as the One who holds the world in God's hands. This idea can remind one of Goethe's words,

God is the East!
God is the West!
Northern and Southern lands
Rest peacefully in his hands.[2]

From the letters contained in the Latin word *tenet*, which is so central here, the words *et te, et te* can also be extracted, which translates as "you too, you too." This sentence thus expresses the central message of the Lord's Prayer, namely, that the Father's love holds everything in God's hands from beginning to end, even you, you too.

This awareness of security is deeply ingrained in the human heart. It can express itself suddenly at very different times and in very different places. This is particularly beautiful in Eduard Mörike's poem *Zum neuen Jahr* ("A Poem for the New Year"), the second verse of which hung framed as a blessing on the wall in my childhood home. The "wheels" (*rotas*) of the Sator Square become sun wheels and circling starry orbits here, the hands that hold are extended to steering and turning; even the "Alpha and Omega" is mentioned here as "Beginning and End," and the Great Sower is called Father.

May the New Year begin in Him
Who moves
Moons and suns
In the blue firmament.
O Father, counsel us!
Lead us and guide us!
Lord, let all things,
Beginning and End,
Be entrusted into Thy keeping![3]

Two things, therefore, are hidden in our magic square.

First, the paternal name of God and second, through the reference to alpha and omega, its eternal validity across all time. Ranier Maria Rilke, the great German poet, gives this image an extraordinarily dynamic interpretation:

> What do I call you? Look, my lips are lame.
> You are the Beginning that gushes forth,
> I am the slow and fearful Amen,
> That timidly concludes your beauty.[4]

Here, "Beginning" also becomes a name of God. The "Amen" that responds is all of us—you and I, the whole of humanity, indeed the entire cosmos—who unfold the radiant beauty of the Beginning in the holy awe of worship in an ever-more astonishing way. The poets quoted here did not, of course, know the Sator Square, but we can discover their mystical insights within the square. And all those who find joy in this ever-mysterious symbol will always find new secrets encoded in it, as I can testify from experience.

A "LOOM OF PRAYER"

THE STRUCTURE OF THE LORD'S PRAYER

Our Father, who art in heaven,
Hallowed be thy name.
Thy kingdom come.
Thy will be done on earth as it is in heaven.
Give us this day our daily bread.
And forgive us our trespasses, as we forgive those
who trespass against us.
And let us not fall into temptation,
But deliver us from evil.
Amen.

Paying attention to the hidden basic structure of the Lord's Prayer can be a great help to us while praying. We do not just have a simple list of seven petitions before us, but the way they are arranged and related to each other is highly artistic.

First of all, the central axis of the Lord's Prayer is the intersection between the invocation "Father" and the petition for daily bread. This intends to evoke the central image for this prayer: the Father as the Giver of bread for God's entire household. This is not just about my daily bread, but our daily bread, and about the whole world as God's household.

The Our Father is a communal prayer; even if we pray it alone, it is always in the name of the whole human family.

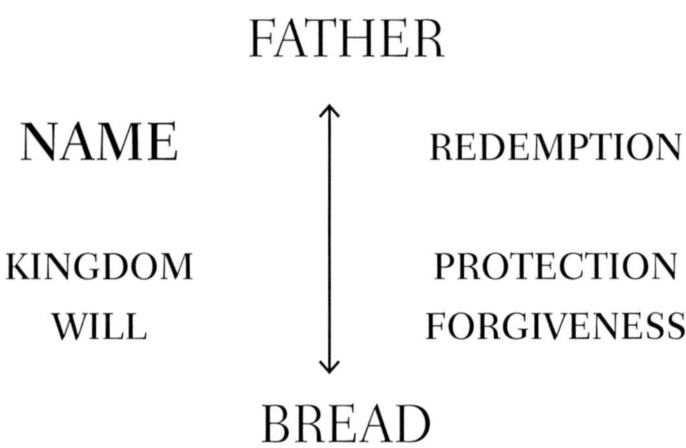

The petition for bread is not the only petition that is intimately connected to "Our Father." Each of the petitions unfolds something that is already contained within the words "Our Father." Name, kingdom, and will are each directly related to the word "Father." The name of the Father contains everything that constitutes God's fatherhood. God's kingdom comes when we live as children of the Father. That also means that we are doing the Father's will in loving obedience. We are therefore invited to weave our lives according to the pattern of this prayer by building God's kingdom and doing God's will on the basis of God's name.

The last three petitions of the Lord's Prayer are also closely linked to the term "Father." Forgiveness is an insepa-

A "Loom of Prayer"

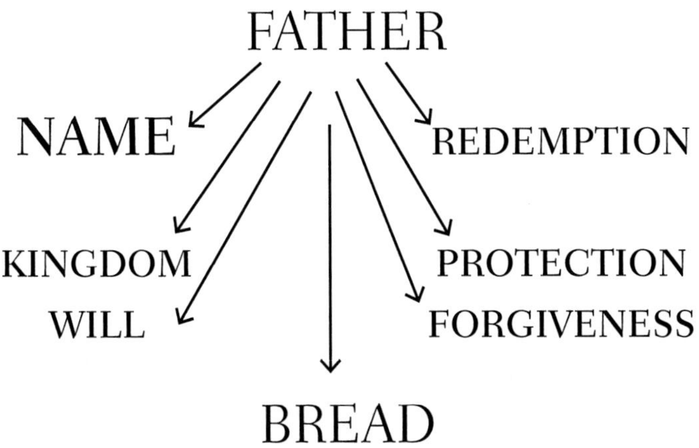

rable part of Jesus's image of the Father; recall the parable of the Prodigal Son. And then there is protection from temptation; what father would not protect his child from danger? How much more does this apply to our Father in heaven when we are tempted! To make this clearer, we have used the translation "Let us not fall into temptation," following the official Spanish and French translations used in churches in those countries.[5] The connection with the Father is also clear when it comes to the keyword "deliverance." Deliverance—"liberation" might be a better translation today—consists simply in the fact that we recognize ourselves as children of the Father and live accordingly in the "freedom of the children of God" (Rom 8:21).

Three requests stand on both sides of the vertical axis connecting the name "Father" with the petition for bread. Now we can see that the requests on the left-hand side are connected to the corresponding requests on the right-hand side by horizontal axes. The most obvious connection is between the petitions that God's will be done and that we forgive as God forgives us. The similarity of the sentence structure of the two petitions makes this clear. God's will is also done on earth, just as it is done in heaven when we forgive our earthly debtors, just as God has forgiven all our debts, even before we became entangled in them.

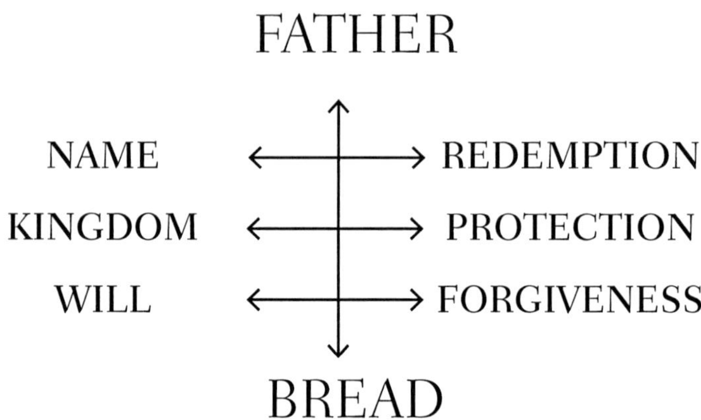

The connection between the requests for the coming of God's kingdom and protection from temptation may not seem quite as clear as the connection between the fulfillment of God's will and the forgiveness of sins, but nevertheless, they are connected.

Every temptation is ultimately a temptation to rebel against God's rule and reign, that is, God's kingdom. In order to understand that the glorification of God's name is also synonymous with our deliverance from all evil, we only have to recall the well-known words of St. Irenaeus, "The glory of God is a human being fully alive." Being delivered from evil means to be liberated to the fullness of life.

As we look at the individual diagrams, the wealth of connecting threads becomes ever richer before our eyes. Now we can also see that the three petitions on either side of the central axis are also connected to each other. Indeed, each one progressively unfolds the other. In our diagram, this connection can be seen in the first three petitions in a descending order and in the last three in ascending order.

FATHER

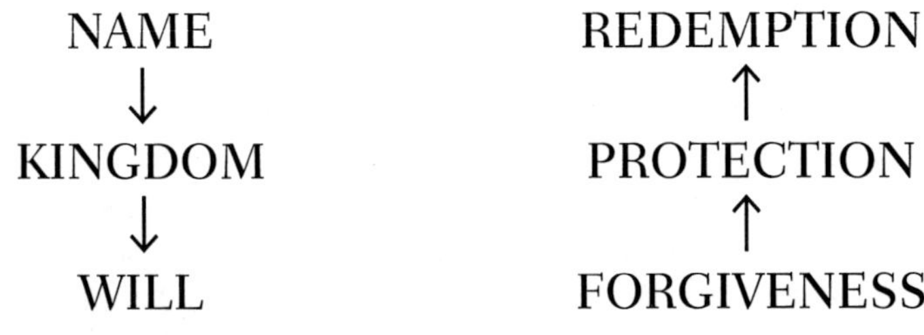

BREAD

Let us first look at the left side. The sanctification, glorification, or hallowing of the NAME "Father," is shown by the fact that God's reign is asserting itself; that God's KINGDOM is coming. That, in turn, means that God's WILL is happening. On the right side of our central axis, the movement is upward: FORGIVENESS heals our relationship to the Divine Mystery, PROTECTION guards and preserves this mutual love when it is in danger, and DELIVERANCE completes it.

I noticed this pattern after the praying the Our Father for years, and in following this pattern, many things slowly became clear to me. There are many indications that the author of the Gospel of Matthew deliberately gave the Lord's Prayer this structure. In the Gospel of Luke, the Lord's Prayer has a similar but shorter form. There are no significant differences in terms of content between the two versions. On the one hand, this suggests that both draw from the same source, a kind of original version of the Lord's Prayer. On the other hand, each author reproduced the form of the prayer that had developed in his own community at that time, namely, around forty years after Jesus's death. However, the chiastic structure of both versions is striking.

The term "chiastic" comes from the Greek letter chi, which resembles our "X" and means "crosswise." In technical language, "chiastic" refers to a pattern of words or sentences that are related to each other but arranged in an A-B-B-A structure. This can make a phrase particularly memorable. For example, the saying "Who dotes, yet doubts, suspects, yet strongly loves"[6] or Goethe's line from Faust, "The world is big, small is the mind."[7]

WHEN THE GOING GETS TOUGH

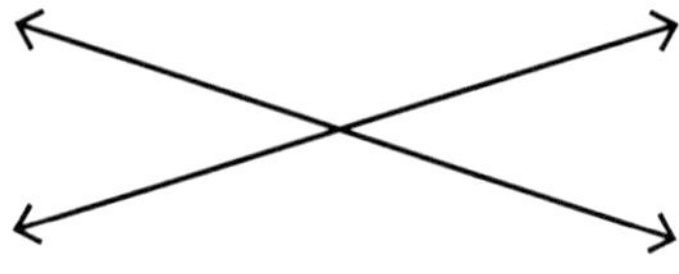

THE TOUGH GET GOING[8]

This chiastic form was very popular in antiquity to achieve a more expressive saying. It is also used here in the Lord's Prayer. The fact that the petition for bread occurs at the intersection of the seven chiastic petitions of the prayer places special emphasis upon it. Because "bread" here means everything we need in the broadest sense, this central petition also includes everything we pray for in the other petitions.

The richness of the interwoven relationships that open up to us this way of looking at things can feel almost overwhelming. I would advise all those who feel this danger to fear not. The only thing that ultimately matters in this prayer is that we open our hearts to God's fatherly love. Even if we do not get beyond the first two words, the loving invocation "Our Father!" sums up everything else and is itself enough. But all those who enjoy weaving the many different patterns on this "loom of prayer," as St. Brigid once called this structure, will certainly feel enriched as they explore the many pairs and patterns it contains.

REFLECTIONS ON THE PETITIONS OF THE LORD'S PRAYER

OUR FATHER IN HEAVEN

Father? "Shall I call You Father? That would mean separating myself from You a thousand times," writes Rilke in *The Book of Pilgrimage*. Even today many feel that the "Father-relationship" is something burdensome that separates them from God. But Jesus Christ recognized You as a Loving Presence, a Great Mystery, and called You "Abba, Father," whereas I would rather call You "Mother."

Since then, countless people have called on You as their Father. May I reverently join that vast multitude. I enter into their venerable community when I also dare to make this prayer my own.

Teach my heart to disregard words where they stand in my way, and to use them as stepping stones when they can help. Do not let me get stuck on any of Your countless names when I stand praying in Your presence. For You are, and remain, the Mystery above all names. Amen.

Father, when we call You that, many people recall disturbing childhood memories of a threatening domestic bully. May we let go of such terrifying images. May we also feel free to call upon You as "Our Mother who art in heaven." Is this not part of the "freedom of the children of God?"

When we pray in community during a church service, it is better to stick to the usual form, because it expresses our reverence for the tradition that connects and unites us. The heartbreaking words of a young man in prison help me, "God is like the father you'd wished you'd had." I am also reminded of Rembrandt's depiction of the *Return of the Prodigal Son*, which can be seen in the Hermitage Museum in St. Petersburg. The painter's deep gaze gave the figure bending over the son two different hands, a strong male one and a more delicate female one. Yes. I say "Amen" to that.

Father, it is often easier for me to call on You as Mother. The Parable of the Merciful Father helps me to better understand this name and this relationship. After all, the father in the parable is much closer to our image of a mother than the traditional image of a father. Like a mother standing at the window, he sees his son coming from afar. When would a father have time for such a lookout?

In the parable, the father says almost exactly what I remember my mother saying, "You need a clean shirt!" Immediately, he has someone bring a festive garment. "You look completely starved!" A feast is already being served. But before all this, the first thing he does is embrace the returning son. Yes, this initial loving embrace is the most special thing of all—and it is deeply maternal. I want to hold on to it, rely on it. Amen.

Father or Mother; both are daring invocations. Whichever one I choose, I am not so much saying something about You, but about myself. I dare to call myself Your child. Yes, I know that You are inwardly closer to me than I am to myself, You are the Source of my being. The image of Father or Mother expresses in shattering clarity "that I am related to You / In a thousand ways,"[9] as Rilke poetically puts it.

"**Our Father**," we say. This reference to community

applies even when I pray all alone. The Lord's Prayer is always the prayer of a community—a boundless community. Are not all living beings Your children? Are we not all sisters and brothers to one another? There is a great deal included in this little word "our."

I'm not just standing in front of You with "all those silent companions in the winds of the meadows."[10] It's not so harmless. There are snakes in the grass, leeches in the pond, and annoying mosquitos all around. Nor can I forget the all-too-many human children of Yours who spit poison, suck blood, or are nuisances to me in so many other ways. It takes courage to see and treat them all as sisters and brothers. I sincerely want to try. Give me the strength to do so. Amen.

Our Father, yes, some people make it really difficult for me to include them in that community that the word "our" presupposes. But aren't there many others whose fellowship I am hardly worthy of myself? Sisters and brothers who patiently, day after day, do what I only talk about? Parents who sacrifice themselves for their children; teachers who reap so little thanks in their arduous profession; all those who risk their health, safety, and lives in service of the sick; immigrant laborers who, often hungry and thirsty themselves, still harvest the fields and provide us all with food.

How dare I stand next to them? Only with great humility. Humility as an awareness of my unworthiness, but also humility in the original sense of the German word for it: *Demut*, which comes from *Dien-Mut*, or "service-courage." I will serve courageously as best as I can. Amen.

Our Father, as often as I call on You by this name, I thank You for the honor of being able to enter into the community of creation, of all Your children. I want to show my gratitude for this belonging by thinking at least once in a while of those who are so often overlooked and whose voices are not heard:

the chronically ill, those who are silenced by society, prisoners in solitary confinement or on death row whose horrific torture is not even recognized as such, the countless children who grow up in inhumane conditions, victims of violence and who never receive justice, missing children and adults.

But above all—and with joyful gratitude—to the billions of unrecognized people who spread courage every day simply by smiling. As the Austrian playwright Franz Grillparzer wrote, "The truly strong are those who laugh through tears, hiding their own suffering to bring joy to others." May I be counted among them. Amen.

Our Father, the circle that this "our" encompasses grows ever wider for me. It does not only encompass the present. As often as I stop and gather myself to pray, I stand in the Now, which spans all times. That is why gathering myself grants me access to the assembly of all Your children.

Shoulder to shoulder with this vast multitude, I too may call upon You as the Father of us all. Today I think of Mary Magdalene and stand beside her in prayer. Tomorrow it may be Joan of Arc on her funeral pyre, or someone recently murdered in the electric chair. Is praying like this a game? Certainly. But isn't praying with words always playful? And You are playing along. I want to take that game seriously. Amen.

In heaven. What should I imagine this to be? I suppose I could start with the dome of the sky that arched over my childhood on the beach at Grado in Italy: blue like gentian flowers, filled with sunlight, vast, and carefree. Or with the starry night sky of my youth: pure, clear, and vaulted infinitely above the damp smell of earth and the smoke of burning campfires—an awesome, inspiring sky.

Later, we experience ourselves "face to face with the sky"—Rilke was sensitive to this—as we lay down on the slope of the spring hill, "among the flowers, face to face with the sky."[11]

Jesus also experienced the sky above his homeland before he could call You "Father in heaven." So too I want to let the heaven that I see above the clouds determine what heaven means to me. Amen.

In heaven. Tens of thousands of years ago, our ancestors imagined Your dwelling place in the sky. Maybe this was because the sky seems both near and far to us—like You, the Mysterious Presence. Nothing separates us from the cloudy sky and yet it is completely inaccessible to us—at least it was inaccessible to us before there were space flights. But we also meet You on such flights. The mocking statement, often attributed to Yuri Gagarin, "I see no god up here" was actually created by the Soviet Party rather than the cosmonaut himself.

In contrast, the American astronaut Rusty Schweickart told me in a trembling voice about those few moments in which a jammed camera interrupted the Apollo 9 mission and he—free-floating outside the capsule, hurtling through space at 25,000 miles per hour—finally found enough peace to be touched by You, the Great Mystery. This great experience now resonates in my mind whenever I say "heaven." I am grateful to You and to Rusty for that. Amen.

In heaven. Being there must mean much more than floating in space. Your heaven cannot be a place; You cannot be located. Wherever I turn to You, You are present to me. And wherever You are present, there is heaven. Your presence is still similar to the blue sky, separated from us by nothing, yet unreachable. Unattainable, not because You are withdrawn, but because we build up things between You and us—images, names, plans. Whatever we build separates us from You and hinders us.

This also applies to the booths at the Jewish festival of Sukkot. That is why they should be "roofed so thinly that the sky shines through." Otherwise, You interfere. Joseph von Eichendorff, the German poet, writes:

It is You who gently breaks down
What we have built above us,
So that we can see heaven—
Therefore, I do not complain[12]

And if that's the way it has to be, I say Amen. The poem all comes down to the last line. I don't just submit to the breaking down of what we build as if "that's the way it has to be." I submit because I trust that it is a loving Father who is behind everything and who lets us see heaven through the holes in the roof. The one we call "Our Father" is the one who does this. That gives me lifelong confidence. I thank You for that. Amen.

In heaven. We hope for our deceased in heaven and pray that they may "rest in peace, having returned to the womb from which they came into this world." That means that our entire journey through life is a return to You. I, too, am on my way home to You—right now, not just at the end of my life. Dorothy Day was right when she said, "All the way to heaven is heaven." How often do I have to say to myself, as the seventeenth-century, priest, poet, and mystic Angelus Silesius wrote, "Stop, where are you going? Heaven is within you." You are "closer to me than I am to myself." "We poor sons and daughters" just have to play our roles to the end. The late eighteenth-century poet Matthias Claudius expressed this so well in his classic "Abendlied" ("Evening Song"):

Grant that, without much grieving,
This world we may be leaving
In gentle death at last.
And then do not forsake us,
But into heaven take us,
Lord God, oh, hold us fast![13]

FATHER? MOTHER?

HEAVEN, HELL, AND PURGATORY

David: When we take such a time-honored prayer as the Our Father upon our lips, we are no longer alone in the moment, but we pray as part of a community that not only encompasses the whole world, but the whole history of the world.

Brigitte: But doesn't that only apply to people who belong to the Christian tradition?

David: That's a very important objection. You are right, the Lord's Prayer first and foremost unites the sisters and brothers of the Christian confessions. But we must not forget that all people of all times come from the Great Mystery, even if they do not call it "Father." Therefore, this prayer not only unites Christians, but the community of all people, because God is the Father of us all.

Brigitte: In our patriarchal world, the image of a father is difficult for me. However, I can empathize very well with my ideal image of a motherly father.

David: I personally concentrate on the awareness of the loving embrace in this prayer. Then all other images recede, so that the image of father and mother merge completely into one another. Jesus uses a very loving word, "Abba," that we translate as "father." It was not unknown in his Jewish tradition but was used less frequently as an invocation of God than, for example, "King" or "Almighty." If Jesus lived in our time, the word "mother" would probably seem more liberating to him than the word "father." Language and consciousness change over the course of history and perhaps it won't be long before we officially translate the first two words in the Lord's Prayer as "Our Mother."

Brigitte: What's so special about Jesus and his "incarnation" that we call him God's "only begotten" Son?

David: Everything special about Jesus Christ is not attributed to him privately, but to him as the representative of all humanity. "Only begotten" does not mean "only child," but God's uniquely beloved Son. Parents love every one of their children as if they were the only one. God loves every one of us as if each one of us is the only beloved child. This should be our ideal for our fellow humans as well. In the Gospel of Luke, Adam, the archetypical human being, is referred to as the "son of God" (Luke 3:38). In the beautiful imagery of the biblical creation myth, God breathes the breath of life into the human, who is made in God's own image. As Genesis describes it, "And the man became a living being."

Could the truth that every human being is a daughter and son of God be expressed any more clearly than in the incarnation? Jesus Christ shows in a unique way what being a child of God means for us all.

Of course, the expression "child of God" remains just an analogy, an image. After all, we can only speak using such images when we consider our origin from the Great Mystery. But as soon as we begin to understand these images of "child of God" and "incarnation" as univocal terms, they become stumbling blocks to us. The very fact that we say "human" and mean an individual illustrates this. In biblical thought, "human" means primarily the whole human race.

Brigitte: You have often spoken about the fact that our sisterhood and brotherhood also extend to animals. But we have very different relationships with them.

David: But different relationships are still relationships and being in relationship means belonging together. The word "our" in "Our Father" includes both friends and enemies.

Brigitte: So the word "Father" unites us into one big family. Unfortunately, we forget that too often.

David: Or we don't even want to admit it.

Brigitte: Part of the concept of family means that we can't choose our family members.

David: And yet, what a great gift it is to belong to such a large and diverse family. As soon as I gratefully accept this gift, I experience the joy of my brotherhood and sisterhood with all creatures. After all, we all live under the same heaven. And this heaven constantly gives us reason to rejoice in its incessant changes. Rilke describes this aptly in his poem "Evening in Skåne":

> Is that one sky?
> Blue—bright, holy—
> Through which pure clouds ceaselessly pour;
> And under it, all is white and passing on;
> And above it, a great curtain of grey,
> Red welling through it as in counterpoint;
> And over all, the silent, broken rays
> Of the sinking sun.[14]

The natural sky in all its ever-changing shades, forms, and colors reminds us of our heavenly Father. Our faithful

Father in heaven never loses sight of us. God knows when and where we stray, finds us, and lovingly leads us home to our Father. There certainly is hell—we know that from our own experience. Who can't relate to the image of a child standing alone in a corner at a party, filled with spite and stubbornness? That child may have already forgotten how she got into that hellish situation. Now she wants to get out, but she can't. Finally, something happens that breaks the spell of emotions. Any explanation of hell should be based on such experiences. Even for the child in the story, this hell is the hopelessness into which we can fall into and lose ourselves. God's almighty, fatherly love, however, ensures that we can find a way out and that hell remains empty.

Brigitte: And how do you understand the term "purgatory?"

David: The best image is probably that of earthly suffering. We must admit that suffering is an inseparable part of life. Even children can understand that you can suffer "with the grain" or against it. Suffering with the grain means that we can overcome suffering by allowing it to scrape away everything that is inauthentic, so that our true loving self can emerge ever purer. The concept of reincarnation is an attempt to explain this mystery. However, such speculations are often only a distraction from our life in the here and now. It is essential to live in peace with ourselves and all others. This means being ready for all the ups and downs of life and accepting them as catalysts for our growth. The gospel speaks of "life in abundance."

Brigitte: The poem "Whoever Hears the Butterflies Laugh" says:

> Whoever lives in peace with himself
> Will die in the same way

And is even more alive
Than all his heirs.[15]

These beautiful lines of poetry are often wrongly attributed to the eighteenth-century German writer known as Novalis. They were actually written in 1973 by Carlo Karges, a founding member of the German rock band Novalis. He was inspired by the earlier poet's work, especially the poem "The Meadow Turned Green."

David: The more alive we become, the more clearly we experience this. Dorothy Day (quoting St. Catherine of Siena) has said, "All the way to heaven is heaven." She cared for the poorest of the poor in the slums of New York. Her friendship was one of the greatest gifts of my life. If anyone was familiar with hell on earth, it was certainly this saintly woman. Yet, you could almost see that she was already in heaven.

Our intimate and heartfelt relationships with friends and relatives turn earth into heaven. This applies not only to our relationships with people but also to our relationships with animals. Should death be able to change this? We already experience every relationship in pure love as "heaven on earth." To the extent that our heart is connected in love with the Father in heaven, we are already there.

HALLOWED BE THY NAME

Your name? Can we really dare to call You by Your name? Wouldn't that mean categorizing You in our understanding of the world—You who are beyond any categories or framework? We understand the world by giving things names. A child names a dog the "Woof-Woof." We name one bird a screech owl and another a cuckoo.

"We, with a word or a finger-sign, / gradually make the world our own,"[16] says Rilke. Initial impressions give us access to everything we name. This is how we grasp our world, at least in part. But how absurd is this to try on You. How could I dare to drag You into the light of conceptual clarity through a name, "You, Darkness, of whom I am born."[17]

Continue to meet me in the darkness of Your incomprehensibility and in the silence of my emotion. Amen.

Your name must rise of its own accord from that depth in which we stand silently before You, the Unspeakable Mystery, and admit Your unnameability. No name can capture You. This insight should resonate with every name we give You, so that we deny it as soon as we say it.

I may only call You Father as long as I do not forget this. Your name as Father was the fruit of silent prayer, which Jesus repeatedly drew himself into in solitude. I too only want to give You the name "Father" out of silence—and immediately let it fade away again into the silent abyss of Your holy presence. This is certainly part of what it means to "hallow" Your name. Therefore, it is only with deep reverence that I will hesitatingly dare to call You Father, O Nameless One. Amen.

Your name—Father—is the first word of the Lord's Prayer in its original language. This name expresses the earth-shattering experience of Jesus, that You are turned toward us in love, O Deepest Mystery. Everything that was important to Jesus, everything that he lived and died for, Your centrality in the world, and our relationship to You and to one another, is derived from the Father's name. Jesus's heartfelt concerns find expression in this prayer. How could it be otherwise?

At first glance, this seems obvious to me. However, I should examine each request in this prayer to see how it is connected to the fact that we call You "Father." I will try to do that, because there is much more to this name than I was previously aware of. Give me insight. Amen.

Your name must be more than a designation. It must go far beyond conceptual comprehension and categorization. Thus, the poet says, "A thousand theologians dived / into the old night of Your name"[18]—to find ever new names that surpass mere naming. "You edge Yourself darkly into mouths, / and with the feeling of having found something / they all surround You with splendor." Being "surrounded with splendor" here probably means praising.

"Praising, that's it!" I think. Each of these divers brings up and into the light a mouthful of new images of praise from the old night of the depths. Who are these "theologians" if not our poets? They are the finders of names: "Neighbor God," "Ancient Tower," "Gentlest Law," "Great Homesickness,"

"Bridge Across All." Such names are not meant to capture. They praise, they "hallow." Jesus likely had such praise of the Father's name in mind. That is how I also want to pronounce that name. Amen.

Hallowed—sanctified, made holy—can mean many things when it refers to Your name. First of all, we probably need to take back every name that we pronounce upon You in order for us to "hallow" Your unpronounceable name. That makes sense to me. Each of Your names must come out of silence and sink back into silence to be "hallowed." This is poetic and almost playful, like the pet names that lovers invent for each other again and again.

However, I am also slowly realizing that the real "holiness" of Your name must be the action that results from naming. When I call You our Father, I must also recognize all of Your children as my siblings. Even that is not enough. I also have to treat them as such. I will have to deal with this in more detail. My actions should correspond more and more to my prayers. Amen.

Hallowed will be Your name through loving action. I am becoming more and more aware of this. The name Father is connected to Your name "Abba," a Father that shows an almost Motherly love. If I dare to call You that, O Incomprehensible Mystery, then I am crossing the threshold into a sacred space where I know the universe as a world hallowed by Your love, O Father of all worlds.

To call You Father means to call You Love. This universe, in which I may stand before You, is a sanctuary of Your love. You are the loving "Yes" that gives every being its existence, myself included. In gratitude, my whole life should also become a "Yes," a boundless affirmation of my belonging to You and—because of You—to everything that exists, because it is Yours as well. Amen.

Hallowed. Only loving energy can hallow Your name, since You are love itself. But my love is lukewarm. Where should I start? First, I can start where my compassion flares up spontaneously, when children suffer. How can I give children that "Yes" of active love that bears Your name? Here, too, I can only think of one initial step: I must not forget them.

I want to focus specifically on their suffering and wrap them in the warmth of my heart as I pray, as if I could hold them in my arms. Children digging for food on garbage heaps in cities, refugee children in distress at sea, enslaved children in their unspeakable homesickness, shivering and freezing child soldiers, children mutilated by landmines, children going blind from malnutrition, unwanted yet still unborn children.

Just holding them in my heart is not enough. I want to help them actively. But how? Make me resourceful. Amen.

Hallowed. In Your name, I can put my name on a petition, support a relief effort, participate in a rally, if it means a "Yes" to the worldwide household of which You are the loving Father.

But Your family includes everyone—yes, even arms dealers, human traffickers, and the smugglers who let refugees drown. In order to let Your name be hallowed, to sanctify Your name, I must learn to love them too. We belong together as brothers and sisters. In the awareness of our community, I also want to say "Yes" to loving them, "Yes" to loving our enemies. I am not indifferent to them. I send them the warmth of my heart. They too were once children and will remain God's children for the rest of their lives. However, I want to oppose their goals with all my strength. This also is part of the hallowedness, the sacredness, of Your name. I will do it courageously and imaginatively. Amen.

MY FAVORITE NAME FOR GOD IS "SURPRISE"

David: It seems to me that all the names we give to the Nameless Mystery want to do just what I mentioned earlier—praise God. All our names for God are like stained glass images in church windows. The daylight that shines through is the Great Mystery in its nameless presence.

Brigitte: Doesn't every name I use to invoke the mysterious reflect my own personal worldview?

David: That is inevitable and expected. Just as we need points of reference for all names, so too with the names of God. The great diversity of human experience gives rise not only to the names of God, but to the very conception of any god. In Hinduism, for example, "Agni" is the god of fire, the "fire form" of the Divine Mystery that emerged from the deepest experience of fire.

Brigitte: It seems liberating to me that we are allowed to understand what others have called "evil idols" as "relatives" of our names of God.

David: This perspective helps me to experience as unifying what is otherwise often seen as divisive.

Brigitte: The most profound connection is that which underlies both these "idols" and the names of God.

David: I cannot distinguish any difference between the emotion I felt in front of the image of the Hindu god Shiva in Chidambaram, India, and the emotion I sometimes feel when praying the Our Father. Therefore, we should always be able to make the name of God—Father—our own and pray it with praise. We can even keep inventing new names for God ourselves. My own favorite name for God is "Surprise."

Historically, we know that Jesus expressed his relationship to the Great Mystery with the word "Abba," Father. From this relationship arose everything that became decisive for his message, his life, and the Christian tradition. If God is our loving Father, then we can live full of trust. That's the very heart of Christian living. Having a common Father makes all living beings sisters and brothers. Acting accordingly transforms all our relationships entirely, in a way that is revolutionary to the world around us. Through everything he did, Jesus showed that the name of God is sacred to him. He lives and died for the kingdom of God. He does the will of God. He becomes bread for all, in the same sense in which my Zen teacher Shunryo Suzuki Roshi would say, "If I let you, you will eat me."

Brigitte: It's the same for everyone who is open to others—open with their eyes, ears, mind, and heart.

David: Jesus also translated the intentions of the other petitions in the Our Father into daily life in a revolutionary way. He prays, "Father, forgive them" for his murderers. In his temptation, he rejects world domination and voluntarily chooses to become the slave to all. This is how he brings about our "deliverance," or our liberation from slavery to the prevailing world order. Every time we pray the Our Father, we begin a path of praxis. Each petition in this prayer points to a very specific step on this path. In this way, the prayer makes us stronger by strengthening our resolve to put the Lord's Prayer into practice in our daily lives. The Lord's Prayer strengthens our "Yes" to togetherness with people from very different backgrounds. This "Yes" means "I am here for you." And it needs to be affirmed—not always in words, but always clearly and energetically. When this is lacking, I not only desecrate my fellow human beings, but also the name of God. I prevent God's name from being hallowed. After all, all of our names for God are summarized in our lives.

Nothing brings more joy to the world than when we share our lives and connect with one another. Bringing joy into the world means sanctifying God's name, letting God's name be hallowed. Nothing brings us more joy than when we bring joy to others. Even a loving word can be a great gift.

Brigitte: If I understand you correctly here, then we hallow God's name through everything that serves life. Everything that destroys life, on the other hand, desecrates it.

David: That's right. We call God the Great Mystery in the innermost heart of life. God's name is Fullness of Life.

Brigitte: Then could we not almost say that God's name is "Nonviolence" as well?

David: Not just almost, just actually and obviously. That's why it's inexplicable to me how billions of people can pray the Lord's Prayer every day without billions of cries going up against the so-called defense industry. We dread and prosecute murderers, but yet we are always building new tools to kill one another with.

Brigitte: Rainer Maria Rilke unites the first murder to the dishonoring of God's name. He says:

I read it here in Your very word,
In the story of the gestures

With which Your hands cupped themselves
Around our becoming—limiting, warm.

You said live out loud, and die You said lightly,
And over and over again You said be.

But before the first death came murder.
A fracture broke across the rings You'd ripened,
A screaming shattered the voices

That had just come together to speak You
To make of You a Bridge
Over the chasm of everything

And what they have stammered ever since
Are fragments
Of Your ancient name.[19]

David: In a world of murder, we find only shards of God's name. But everything we do to heal and bring life becomes the sanctification of God's name.

THY KINGDOM COME

Your kingdom and what that really means can only be really understood if we consider the historical situation in which this prayer arose. Jesus and his disciples were Jews, violently oppressed and exploited by the Roman occupying forces. The request for Your kingdom only gains its full power in contrast to the violent empire of the Romans.

Realizing Your kingdom on earth, and doing so without violence, was Jesus's great passion. He lived for this and was put to death for this. The kingdom of God stood against the Roman Empire. Political rulers sense something like this immediately. They recognized the competition and attacked. No one has ever been crucified for nonpolitical altruism. The more sincerely I inherit Your kingdom, the more energetically I must be prepared to stand up for it—even politically. Give me the courage to do so and take away my fear of the consequences. Amen.

Your kingdom is "not of this world." It's not like any kind of world empire. Rather, it is the kingdom of peace that every human heart longs for. We can see this in our nature, as Your worldwide household. We must first realize this through the free "Yes" of love before we can truly see this in our societies. For You do not impose Your order upon us. You are a Father, not a ruler by force.

And yet, You are repeatedly depicted "upon the highest throne" of a hierarchical power structure. Although this is a sincere attempt to honor You, it is also heartbreaking blasphemy. Jesus understood Your kingdom precisely as the antithesis of such a power structure; one not based on conquest, but on new ways of thinking; not based on fearmongering, but on mutual trust; not realized through violence, but without violence. In other words, not of this world, but in the midst of it. Amen.

Your kingdom, as Jesus understood it, is not a demarcated area of dominion "here or there," but "among" us. You have given us this possibility, which we can make into reality if we only want to. Your "dominion"—the power of Your love—is available to us at all times. An opportunity to say "Yes" to each other is always at hand. Your kingdom is the joyful life together that emerges when a community begins to dance to Your music. Just "two or three" are enough to start, such as two lovers who start a family together, or three friends who form the seed of a community. And how can we recognize Your kingdom? In living love. In the fact that people can feel at home unconditionally and know that their independence is respected. In other words, in human dignity. Awaken in me the attentive willingness to work for this. Amen.

Your kingdom does not only mean the heavenly glory that we hope for when pray for our deceased loved ones to "enter into Your kingdom." The Indian mystic Kabir puts it bluntly:

> The idea that the soul will join with the ecstatic
> Just because the body is rotten—
> That is all fantasy.

What is found now is found then.
If you find nothing now,
You will simply end up with an apartment in the
City of Death.[20]

Your kingdom is a kingdom of the living, and life and vitality must therefore be its main characteristics, even here on earth.

Of course, everything in this world remains incomplete, including Your kingdom. The guiding principle of our building must extend into the hereafter. As the old saying goes, "What we are here, God will complete there."[21] Now and always, You are and will remain the Intersection of all relationships and the Center of Your kingdom. The poet's words apply, "With each disclosure you encompass more / and she stretches beyond what limits her, / to hold you."[22] Amen.

"Thy kingdom **come**," we pray, and that sounds quite passive. However, anytime we have actively shaped our coexistence, throughout the whole of human history, we have scarcely seen the dawning of Your kingdom of peace. As much as we all long for it, we seem to have lost our way completely. The whole thing has gone astray. Is it too late to turn back?

Your kingdom must be a gift. After all, You give us everything there is. But like every other gift, it remains only an offer. It only becomes a real gift when we demonstrate our gratitude by making something of that which is offered.

And that is what countless people do, those who honestly and sacrificially strive to find starting points for completely new forms of living together as sisters and brothers. Let me also recognize such new starting points as Your gifts and use them courageously and gratefully. Amen.

"Thy kingdom **come**," we pray. Yet we know that it's already there, in our midst, as a constant possibility. When

You bring two or three of us together it is also an offer from You to be together "in Your name." After all, Your name is Love, and every encounter is a new opportunity to express the "Yes" of love. With this "Yes," we hallow Your name and receive each other, and thus Your kingdom, with arms wide open. Your name and Your kingdom are therefore germinating whenever and wherever we shape our lives together.

Make us awake and attentive to this sprouting entrusted to us. Let us also patiently nurture the tender seeds of love so that Your kingdom can blossom from them. Amen.

"Thy kingdom **come**" as a social reality! In the order of the cosmos, You act as its Innermost Vitality, "You Most Gentle of Ways." In the earth's household, nature presents us with a living picture of that harmonious life together that Your kingdom—the household of God—wants to give us.

Nature does not build pyramids of power, but interweaves network with network, just as in music where motif interweaves with motif. Wherever we pay reverent attention to nature, You show us models for the design of Your kingdom.

Teach us to follow them in everything we build. Then we can also trust in nature's inexhaustible power of renewal, that it will not only heal the wounds we have inflicted upon it, but also show our culture the way to a healed existence. Amen.

"Thy kingdom **come**." That is what we long for. We know that only You can ultimately fulfill this longing, yet we cannot expect Your kingdom as Your gift without any effort on our part. What do we need to do so that Your kingdom can take place among us? What can I contribute from my tiny sphere?

But my sphere of influence extends further than I often realize. After all, everything is interconnected with everything else! Whenever we do good to each other out of the awareness that we are created for each other, we set in motion an unbreakable "Yes" of love. This impulse continues without limit. As often as we show mutual respect for one another, a spark of the radiance of Your kingdom spreads, shining ever further. Give me strength and determination to contribute to the coming of Your kingdom in this way. Amen.

KINGDOM OF GOD AS A CONCRETE TASK

David: Because God is love, the kingdom of God must be the kingdom of love. We can seek to realize this ideal courageously and energetically in both our private and political lives. Even the Roman Empire presented itself as a kingdom of peace, and indeed, the Pax Romana did provide the Roman Empire with two centuries of relative peace from uprisings and civil wars. This kind of peace, though, was enforced by the love of power. Peace in the kingdom of God, however, is based on the power of love. Power has only one legitimate function, which is to empower the disempowered for good. Unfortunately, the liturgy uses images that place God at the top of a power hierarchy. In doing so, we strive to honor God, but fall into the opposite trap. I am thinking, for example, of hymns such as "Here Before Your Majesty Lies [in the Dust, the Multitude of Christians]."[23]

We all have the same dignity as humans, even though we are each so different. We are unique beings with very different strengths and weaknesses. We can remain aware of this dignity, even in the midst of a world that constantly threatens this awareness. God is not the pinnacle of a hierarchical power pyramid, but the Love that floods an interconnected network as the Breath of Life, holds it together, and shapes it into what we call the "kingdom of God." The more powerful mutual appreciation becomes in a group, the more this community realizes the kingdom of God. This can begin in even the smallest circle. It draws ever wider circles of its own accord—circles of joyful life.

Brigitte: When you say "circles of joyful life," I believe "joy" is the keyword. Joy is contagious. That's why I like your image of what "joyful life together" looks like: a community that begins to dance to the music of God.

David: God's name is music, and the dance of love is God's kingdom. Even though our efforts will always remain incomplete, the hope remains alive that the kingdom of God will at least reach completion beyond time and space. St. Paul says, "What God wants is plain to all people; God made it plain to all. Ever since the creation of the world, the works of creation have expressed God's invisible reality" (freely adapted from Rom 1:19–20). Therefore, in the works of creation, our human reasoning can perceive what God wants. That is a great encouragement to me. So many people who know nothing about Christianity or don't even want to hear about it are nevertheless actively involved in building the kingdom of God. Learning from nature is an essential area in which an astonishing amount of new things are currently taking place. "Bionics" and "biomimetics" are research fields that study and imitate natural systems and structures, in order to solve difficult technical, social, or organizational problems.

Brigitte: Everyone knows some classic examples of technological imitations of nature, such as Velcro, which was inspired by the sticky burs of the burdock plant. There are countless other inventions, though, that are also copied from nature, for example, self-healing bioconcrete which contains bacteria that can close cracks that appear in the concrete. Even some city planners are learning from ants in order to solve organizational problems such as traffic jams. The most important thing, however, is that learning from nature becomes a basic attitude for all of us.

David: Our entire educational system, from kindergarten to college, would have to play a key role in this. At first glance, this might seem quite removed from the Lord's Prayer to some, but it is an essential part of its meaning. Nature sanctifies—hallows—the name of God by showing us what God stands for. If we are prepared to learn from nature without prejudice, we will find the model for the kingdom of God already laid out in seed form. Dante calls love the innermost secret of the universe, "the Love that moves the sun and the other stars."

Brigitte: This is also how I understand Pierre Teilhard de Chardin's famous statement, "Someday, after mastering the winds, the waves, the tides, and gravity, we shall harness for God the energies of love, and then, for a second time in the history of the world, man will have discovered fire."[24]

David: Then the Lord's prayer for the coming of the kingdom of God will have been fulfilled.

THY WILL BE DONE, ON EARTH AS IT IS IN HEAVEN

Your will points in a certain direction, if I understand it correctly. For life, as the innermost essence in which we recognize You, O unfathomable Mystery, life in us and around us has such an orientation. It does not whirl about chaotically but unfolds with an inner order. Specific, individual events may be indeterminate, but we can statistically recognize an orientation toward order. Science proves this as well, despite rejecting any "purposefulness" of evolution.

As always when we play, the goal of the great cosmic dance is not at the finish line, but in the dance itself. Your will is the music of vitality to which everything dances, which we hear within ourselves with the ears of the heart. Make us sensitive to it and give us the joyful willingness to dance unanimously to its rhythm. Amen.

Your will points in the "direction of being alive." Therefore, it must be possible to discern characteristics of Your will from the life of nature and to align ourselves accordingly. As long as something is alive, it is integrated into orderly networks of relationships and resists decay into chaos. Another characteristic of living beings is that they distinguish their inside from their outside, and therefore are autonomous. Life itself flows in one direction: it wants to grow, develop, and multiply.

You also want us humans to realize Your order through our "Yes" to mutual belonging and interconnectedness. This includes joyfully allowing and enabling each other's individuality and self-development. The mutual recognition of our human dignity is the characteristic by which we can recognize whether we are living in harmony with Your will. Let us strive for and achieve this harmony. Amen.

Your will is the complete fullness of the cosmic dance—can it even be expressed in commandments? Can it be fulfilled by the mere observance of commandments? Probably only insofar as commandments instruct us to listen attentively to the beat of the cosmic dance of truth. As soon as something is put into words as a commandment, though, it already belongs to a particular culture, which is reciprocally determined and conditioned with it.

However, the unconditional that lies behind the commandments is audible to every human heart and connects us with one another across all cultural differences. The closer a commandment is to this universally valid ethos, the more binding it is. "Do to others as you would have them do to you" is one such basic rule that we can all agree with. It alone would be enough to transform the order of our world. Give us the courage to do so. Amen.

Your will be done! How could it not be done? Is there anything that can resist Your will? Here is where I discover the secret of my own freedom. I experience that I can choose, and that I always choose what seems desirable to me. I cannot do otherwise. In doing so, I do on my level of consciousness what the single-celled organism does on its own when it strives for that which nourishes life and flees from that which destroys life. On the human level of consciousness, everything depends on the framework of choice; choosing ego or common good, choosing short-term or long-term satisfaction.

Delaying satisfaction is difficult for my impatience, community spirit is difficult for my egoism, and the willingness to try is difficult for my laziness. Let me overcome these resistances. Only when all beings are happy can I also be happy. My lasting happiness is Your will. Let me willingly strive for this great, universal, and lasting happiness, nothing less. Amen.

On earth as it is in heaven is shorthand for contemplation. Since time immemorial, people have tried to establish a relationship with the mysterious order of the starry heavens on earth. Huge prehistoric stone circles, such as those at Stonehenge, still bear witness to this today. Later, such structures developed into temples. Temple architecture is oriented toward the stars because it aims to reflect the order of heaven on earth.

That is the essence of contemplation. It is not idly staring at the sky, but the effort to align human society with heaven like a temple. In this sense, the Lord's Prayer is a contemplative prayer. It expresses the longing for a world order in which a "higher" order—Your order—becomes reality "on earth as it is in heaven." The Christian tradition is contemplative at its core. Give me insight and energy to come ever closer to this ideal. Amen.

On earth as it is in heaven. We can see what this might look like in nature. Heaven is everywhere where Your will is done. And wherever we humans have not yet violated nature, the harmony of an order unfolds which we recognize as Your "will." The contemplative axis that connects seeing and doing runs not only vertically between heaven and earth, but also horizontally between nature and culture.

The keyword for contemplative commitment is "bionics"—the application of what we learn from nature to solving human problems. For billions of years, nature has recycled all waste materials, but we have contaminated the earth and seas in just a few decades. Because I want to pray this Our Father request honestly, I commit myself to doing something about nuclear and plastic waste. Amen.

On earth as it is in heaven. Yes, really, Your will must be done not just here and there, but all over the world if we want to get closer to the "heaven on earth" that we so long for. Our greatest problems are global. We can only solve them together. It is becoming increasingly clear to me that every request in the Lord's Prayer only unpacks what is already contained in the first two words of this prayer. Because You are the Father of us all, everything depends on us moving from "I" thinking to "we" thinking.

Only together can we hope to get violence, environmental destruction, or explosive population growth under control. Most of us do not work in weapons manufacturing. Is it therefore none of our business that mutual slaughter is commonplace in our human family? Who is surprised by weapons manufacturing anyway? Teach us to question the questionable. Amen.

On earth as it is in heaven points to change, to transition, to transformation. All the misery of the earth is to be transformed into the joy of heaven. Christian tradition expresses our hope for this goal in apocalyptic images in which the heavenly Jerusalem comes down from heaven "like a bride adorned for her bridegroom." You will wipe away every tear from our eyes. "Death will be no more; mourning and crying and pain will be no more" (Rev 21:4), for You make all things new.

Yes, but this does not happen without our doing. Anyone who really longs for heaven on earth will not sit around and wait for it but will work toward it with courage. You have put the future in our hands. We shape it through our actions and are thereby transformed ourselves as a result. Grant that we don't run out of breath. Amen.

THE WILL OF GOD IS LIFE IN FULL BLOOM

David: We have seen that the unfolding of life in the universe is striving toward the "kingdom of God." Only holistic thinking makes us aware that every detail of everything we do is part of a purposeful movement.

Brigitte: With each small step we come closer to the goal of a society of brotherly and sisterly love.

David: But not as if the goal is far away. The goal is the realization of God's will in every moment. Just as the fullness of a dance does not come at the end but lies in the fulfillment of each individual dance step.

Brigitte: The will of God is, as you say, the music of vitality. And it is realized when we dance lively to this music, moment by moment.

David: The joy of inner liberation is how we recognize that we are doing God's will.

Brigitte: However, most people probably associate liberation more with freedom from the restrictions that commandments place upon them than obeying such commandments.

David: Hasidic Jewish mystics have made a highly imaginative connection between freedom and commandments. In Hebrew, only the consonants of a word are written. Thus, the same written word can be pronounced and understood in very different ways depending on the vowels used. In the biblical story in which Moses brings the tablets of the law down from Mount Sinai, the usual translation reads, "the law of God, engraved on the tablets." But the Hasidic teachers say, "Do not read 'the law of God, engraved (*harut*) on the tablets,' but rather 'the law of God: freedom (*herut*) on the tablets.'" This means that in a deeper sense, following the commandments does not mean restriction, but freedom. Even the dancers in the round dance are only freed to dance joyfully and uninhibitedly by performing the precise steps.

Brigitte: Commandments are conditioned by culture. But what is the unconditional behind them?

David: We experience the basic ethical orientation, innate to us as human beings, as absolutely binding. The classic example of this is the golden rule, "Do not do to others what you do not want done to yourself." This is just one of the many formulations that express an ethical awareness that we all share. The closer a commandment is to the universally valid ethos, the more binding it is. Unfortunately, there are commandments in all religions that have nothing to do with God's will, but are merely religiously formulated cultural prejudices, such as dietary regulations, purity laws, clothing regulations, and commandments that regulate sexual behavior. There are even commandments that contradict God's will! Such commandments, which are based only on culture, have often contributed to hostilities between people and religions.

Brigitte: How can we talk of God's will in connection with our freedom?

David: A comparison with music might help us here again. I am invited to freely improvise with the music of the cosmos. In doing so, I can adapt attentively, imaginatively, and with dedication to the melodic flow of the whole. But I can also play reluctantly. That will cause dissonances, but the great Conductor has everything under control so that these dissonances are also incorporated immediately. The piece as a whole becomes different as a result, but it remains beautiful.

Brigitte: Are you really taking the "dissonances" you are talking about seriously enough here? These include shocking crimes and historical catastrophes in the world.

David: Yes, we must not trivialize the dissonances under any circumstances. Even missteps that initially seem harmless can trigger avalanches. Every moment in the great dance of life offers us many different possibilities for the next step. We have the choice. This is where our creativity shows itself. But not all steps fit the beat of the dance. This means that we have to be alert; impatience, egoism, and laziness deafen us to the music of life and cause us to fall out of step. Here, stumbling means a lack of freedom.

If a wheel is not properly seated on the axle, it squeaks. Contemplation is the effort to center the wheel of my life again so that it runs in complete silence, even when I'm up to my ears in work. In the midst of noise and hustle and bustle, our heart can remain silent because it is anchored in the eternal Now. For example, when we become quiet and look up to heaven.

Brigitte: I have experienced this many times. Even lively young people become completely silent when they stand in amazement under the starry sky.

David: Such looking up to heaven and projecting the heavenly order onto earth is not just the original meaning of contemplation. "On earth as it is in heaven" is also the contemplative axis around which the entire Lord's Prayer revolves. The Lord's Prayer presents seeing and doing as an axis between heaven and earth. There we see the will of God—the order of love—realized "as it is in heaven." It is depicted in the order of the starry sky, in contrast to the chaos that we create "down here."

Today, the other axis is closer to us, the one between nature and culture. Here we see God's order reflected in nature—for example, in the complete recycling of all materials, in contrast to the chaotic destruction of the environment through poisoning it with garbage. Both axes are necessary for our orientation, both are about seeing and realizing the will of God.

The Our Father takes us from "I" to "we." The word "our" in the Lord's Prayer confronts us with our duties toward our sisters and brothers. This includes questioning exclusion and injustice. For me, questioning is expressed very concretely by asking uncomfortable questions in everyday life. I try to wake others up. Too many crimes in our world are only able to be committed because they are covered up. The Lord's Prayer encourages me to question everything that is questionable in light of the "we" consciousness. Heaven on earth remains an apocalyptic ideal but it should inspire us to work toward it now with all our strength.

Brigitte: This enthusiasm also transforms us.

David: This transformation takes place the moment we connect with one another and work for a more just society. Simultaneously, our joy in doing so is also the fulfillment of the request that God's will be done on earth as it is in heaven. Because God wills our joy.

GIVE US THIS DAY OUR DAILY BREAD

Give us this day our daily bread represents everything we hope for, ask for, and expect from You. We hope for it because we are dependent on it in every respect. We ask for it because we are aware that all human effort is not enough to provide us with the necessities of life. But we can also expect it with full confidence because we know You as our "Father"—as the You who we all have in common at the heart of our being.

The image of the Father is intended to express the love with which You, O Unfathomable Mystery, organize and maintain the world's household, just as the Roman *paterfamilias* kept his household in order, gave the pets their food, and all relatives their daily bread at the right time. Let us never lose the awareness of our dependence on the gifts of life, but rather celebrate it gratefully. Amen.

Our daily bread, received consciously and gratefully, from the giving, joyfully-open hand of life truly fills our hearts with joy at what has been given to us. This completely contrasts with the dull indifference with which we so often thoughtlessly take possession of it, as if it were a matter of course.

This is probably also the reason why Jesus Christ teaches us to ask for what You have long since given us and always give us, even when we do not pray for it. In the same way, mothers teach their little ones to say "please" before giving them a treat. They get the treat anyway, but they only experience real joy when they recognize it as a gift. Make me more and more aware that everything is a gift, and that the meaning of life is the joy of life, evidence that we are genuinely joyful for this gift. Amen.

Our daily bread? Why do we ask for "daily" bread? Nobody knows for sure what the original Greek word that we translate today as "daily" really means. One thing is clear, though, we ask for what is necessary for "today." When we call it our "daily" bread, however, there is also the awareness that we need it not just today, but every day, and indeed, it suggests a trust that we will receive it every day.

Do not let me lull myself into a false sense of security and fall asleep spiritually. I am grateful that I had to experience the fear of starvation firsthand, and I want to pray together with all those who are suffering from hunger today. I look at photos of emaciated children with hungry bellies with deep shame. Keep this shame alive in me so that it becomes the spark for a willingness to help. Amen.

Our daily bread is what I pray for, not mine. You give us bread enough for everyone; it is up to us to make sure that everyone gets their fair share. Ultimately, then, in this petition of the Lord's Prayer, we are not praying for enough bread, but for the active willingness to share it with one another.

Whenever I pray for our daily bread, I realize that I am partly responsible for world hunger. Since I know its horrific extent, but also know that there are reliable ways to eliminate it, I cannot pray for bread for everyone without also working toward this goal. How? Simply speaking about world hunger at every opportunity can strengthen community awareness and the will to work together. Give me the courage to support self-help in poorer countries financially, but also the personal willingness to change my eating habits. Amen.

"THE EARTH GIVES"—AS MUCH AS WE NEED, NOT AS MUCH AS WE WANT

Brigitte: Everything is really a gift, even if we must labor for it, because even the strength to labor is a gift. That is probably what this request is about. Rilke says it so aptly once again:

> In spite of all the farmer's work and worry,
> He can't reach down to where the seed is slowly
> Transmuted into summer. The earth bestows.[25]

David. The image of Mother Earth, who gives us bread, very appropriately complements the image of the Father in heaven as the Giver of all gifts. Both are images of the central axis of giving and receiving in our lives. This is also the central axis in the Lord's Prayer. Ultimately, everything is a gift, even if we must labor for it.

A Buddhist meal blessing says, "Innumerable efforts have given us these gifts; we should be mindful of how they come to us." Unfortunately, our food industry also has its dark side. We torture animals in factory farms and meat-processing plants, and we pollute the soil with overfertilization and the animals with antibiotics. Yes, many of these life-threatening encroachments are caused by our high meat consumption. Just to put a pound of beef on my plate requires almost two thousand gallons of water! When we specifically pray for "our daily bread," then it is about nothing more and nothing less than what we really need. But that is in stark contrast to the "desire to have" that is never satisfied.

Brigitte: I like the fact that the word "daily" already contains a very conscious attitude to life. I have often wondered about the juxtaposition of "this day" and "daily;" it always seemed redundant to me.

David: The Greek word *epiousion*, translated here as "daily," must be important, because both Matthew and Luke use it, although in Luke the whole prayer is shorter. The interesting thing is that in all of the known Greek literature of antiquity, this word only appears here in the Lord's Prayer. The theologian Origen of Alexandria was the first to study the meaning of this word at the beginning of the third century. Although Greek was his native language, he did not know the word, but assumed that it could be translated as "what is necessary for existence."

Brigitte: So we have no comparison in antiquity that could clarify what it means?

David: Correct. But in the Gospel we have at least some clues as to what *epiousion*, which we translate as "daily," could mean in the Lord's Prayer. Immediately after the Lord's Prayer in Matthew there follows the passage that warns against "storing up." "Do not store up for yourselves treasures on earth, where moth and rust consume and where thieves break in and steal; but store up for yourselves treasures in heaven.... For where your treasure is, there your heart will be also" (Matt 6:19–21). It becomes even clearer when Jesus says, in the same chapter, "Do not worry about tomorrow, for tomorrow will bring worries of its own" (Matt 6:34). And in the story of the manna that the Heavenly Father gave to his children in the desert, it is reported that this "bread from heaven" rotted when the Israelites accumulated more of it than they needed for a single day (Num 11:1–9).

Brigitte: That is why Matthias Claudius calls the poem "To Be Sung Daily," in which the well-known verse is found,

> May God only give me every day
> As much as I may, to live on.
> He gives it to the sparrow on the roof,
> How could he not give it to me![26]

David: Deep trust, then. No accumulation—when shopping, in the pantry, at the table. Every single request in the Lord's Prayer demands a lot from us! What Rilke says in his well-known poem named after and referring to "The Archaic Torso of Apollo" also applies to the whole Lord's Prayer: "Here there is no place that does not see you. You must change your life."[27]

AND FORGIVE US OUR TRESPASSES, AS WE FORGIVE THOSE WHO TRESPASS AGAINST US

Forgive us our trespasses. This literally means our "debts," or our "guiltiness." Guilt could come naturally to my tongue at this point. Guilt has something to do with the shame I feel when I ask for my daily bread and know that children are starving at the same time. You give us bread so that we can share it, but our society owes it to the hungry. When we think of "guilt," we usually think of personal guilt when we break a law. But "debt" is not meant to be understood as breaking the law, but rather means above all our remaining indebtedness to others when we justly owe them something.

If we limit "trespasses" to mere violations of regulations, we are making it easy for ourselves, because legal rulings can often be cleverly circumvented with backdoors and loopholes. But if justice means the fair distribution of what we have, then our hearts accuse us when others are deprived of the necessities of life. Our hearts are not so easily deceived. "If you have two coats, you have stolen one from the poor," is a famous saying by the aforementioned Dorothy Day. So let me clearly recognize my debt to all those to whom I owe something, admit it, and make amends as best as I can. Amen.

Forgive us our trespasses, Father, and let us admit what they actually consist of, because that is the first step toward forgiveness. You want us to share everything You give us fairly with one another. Sharing is important to You.

Sharing and forgiveness are closely intertwined. Just as Your just distribution only reaches its goal when we share with one another, so too Your forgiveness only reaches its goal when we forgive one another. A world of just distribution of goods and general forgiveness of debts and guilt would be a world full of peace—that would be Your kingdom and the fulfillment of Your will, on earth as in heaven. Let us long for this goal so ardently that we actually set out on the path. Because where there is a will, there is a way. Amen.

Forgive us our trespasses, I pray. I notice that I often say "trespass" or "debt" but actually mean "sin"—a violation of Your commandment, of Your "will." The fact that I know deep in my heart what You actually want is proven to me by my sense of shame when I see the injustices of this world, where children are starving, and millions are denied a life worthy of a human being. No, You want "life in abundance."

My shame makes me feel that my failure is tearing apart the delicate network through which everything is connected to everything, even connected to You. The word "sin," and its Germanic root *Sünde* come from a word meaning "to separate." Sin means a tear in the fabric of the whole. It separates what belongs together, and that is literally heartbreaking. For the heart is—as Rilke puts it so wonderfully—that which is "born into the whole."[28] If we live from our heart, then we belong to the whole, then we become whole, then we will also absorb what seems so difficult to us about the whole, then we will get along with the whole. The heart is the area where we are most deeply and intimately connected to everything and everyone and to the divine. That is why the heart does not resign itself to separation and urges us to overcome it. But even when our hearts accuse us, we can trust You, because You are "greater than our hearts, and [You know] everything" about us (1 John 3:20). Let me trust in Your limitless forgiveness and pass it on generously. Amen.

Forgive us our trespasses, as we forgive, it continues. Your forgiveness and ours are therefore comparable in some sense. That means, though, that the comparison can also be reversed, and we should forgive as You forgive. Now I ask, "How do You actually forgive?" Debt or guilt is not about legal matters, but about an experience of the heart; I have already realized that. That is why forgiveness must be about more than that as well.

You forgive us not through legal pardon, but through a kind of artistic inclusion of "even sins" in the whole—*etiam peccata*, says Augustine. He calls to us, "Observe the whole, praise the whole."[29] Without glossing over the guilt—my own or that of others—I will try to understand forgiveness in such a way that I strive for nothing other than reparation. Amen.

As we forgive originally meant "as we forgive financial debts." People who prayed like this did not want to elevate themselves above their sisters and brothers as creditors over debtors, since "no one claimed private ownership of any possessions, but everything they owned was held in common" (Acts 4:32). If we pray this petition in the Lord's Prayer as it was originally intended, we shake the foundations of our economic order by showing the limits of the right to private property.

But how can we achieve this without simply dropping out of our society? History offers admirable examples of doing this, from St. Francis to the Amish even today.

And shouldn't we do this as Your children? We owe You everything we have, but You don't write a promissory note, You give it completely unconditionally. Does this petition of the Lord's Prayer really make such radical demands on us? Can we try to transform the whole of society from within? Yes, only in Your strength, for Your sake. Amen.

As we forgive. Everything will depend on how grateful we are for Your "forgiveness." Your forgiveness is also demonstrated by the fact that we have not already destroyed ourselves in spite of all the destruction that we cause every day. When it dawns on us that we owe our survival only to Your "forgiveness," then we cannot help but forgive one another as generously as You do.

How can we start overcoming the mutual destruction that we humans threaten each other with? We must think about the big picture, but I must start on a small scale with that which is needed on a large scale. Where mutual injury requires forgiveness, I have to make a start and cannot wait long for reciprocity. The author Jean Paul Friedrich Richter (1763–1825) said, "Man is never so beautiful as when he begs or grants forgiveness."[30] You give us new opportunities to do this every day. Amen.

As we forgive has to do with giving—with Your giving and with ours. Forgiveness is the ultimate form of giving. The greatest of all the gifts You give us is that You also forgive us when we misuse Your gifts. Forgiveness is shown by the fact that You warn us through events such as climate change and natural disasters, but always give us new opportunities to do better.

Let me forgive like this too, when anger takes hold of me because the powerful are destroying the rainforest and the polar ice caps and I feel so helpless. Anger is powerless, but forgiving love makes one resourceful. With protests in public life and with warmth of heart in private life, I want to contribute to the healing of everything that is wounded, to the reconnection of everything that is torn, and to the revival of what has died. Amen.

As we forgive—the very manner in which we do so will show others and ourselves how seriously we take the Our Father as a whole. We hallow Your name as Father in heaven by forgiving in Your name—in the light of Your name as Father and with the warmth of heart that unites us as children in the divine household of Your kingdom. Only in this way can we fulfill Your will, by forgiving on earth as You forgive in heaven.

But only radiant enthusiasm for Your will can transform accusation into forgiveness, just as glowing heat transforms leaven into bread. Of this light, this warmth, this radiance, Jesus says, "I came to bring fire to the earth, and how I wish it were already kindled!" (Luke 12:49). Our goodwill is not enough. May our hearts burn in Your Holy Spirit! Amen.

"TRESPASSES" AS TEARING, REMAINING GUILTY, AND FALLING OUT OF STEP

David: It's always about resonating with life in its balance of give-and-take. If I fall out of this resonance with life, then I have trespassed. Sin is linguistically related to "separating." Sin means a tear that runs through the fine fabric of our relationships. Such "trespassing" can always be understood as remaining guilty. For me as a Christian, it is very comforting to read in 1 John 3:19-20 that even if our conscience speaks to us of our guilt, we can trust that God is more compassionate towards us than we are towards ourselves. This is how the German Bible translation *Hope for All* reproduces the passage in 1 John, which literally reminds us that "whenever our hearts condemn us...God is greater than our hearts" (3:20).

Brigitte: The ethical counterpart to this is, "To understand everything is to forgive everything."

David: And God—the Great Mystery—is Love. That is why God does not just forgive sins, God is forgiveness. God does not hand out punishments, but gifts.

Brigitte: In our discussions we have repeatedly used the image of dancing to the great cosmic music. The trespass then becomes a misstep, a failure to listen to the music causing an offbeat step.

David: These three images of sin as tearing apart, remaining guilty, and falling out of step also indicate quite clearly how we can make amends for the trespass—by carefully reweaving relationships, by restoring balance to relationships, by attentively listening to the music of life.

Brigitte: And where does the Christian doctrine of "original sin" fit in here?

David: The phrase "original sin" is definitely obsolete, if only because it is simply misleading. The painful experience that led to the idea of original sin is by no means limited to Christianity. Buddhists use the word *dukkha* for this, which originally referred to the image of a wheel with an axle hole drilled off-center. For Buddhists, it means that human existence has been a bumpy, offtrack journey since time immemorial. We are born into this situation. We inherit it, so to speak. Today we might express it, "We participate in the systemic evil of the world, whether we are to blame for it or not!" As individuals, we are no match for the system. That is why the answer that the Christian tradition provides is that you must get out of the deadly system and enter the life-giving kingdom of God.

Brigitte: When it comes to the topic of "guilt" or "debt," you speak of an "experience of the heart." What do you mean by that?

David: We know what "heart" means, right? We talk about something touching our heart, about something stirring our heart, or about giving our heart away. Heart represents our innermost being. We can therefore describe deep, inner experiences as experiences of the heart. We also know what it means to open our heart. And whoever opens their heart has experiences of the heart.

Ultimately, this petition in the Lord's Prayer is about transformation. But not just about transforming guilt into forgiveness, above all, about the deep transformation of the person praying from living with half-heartedness to living with radiant enthusiasm.

When you pray, and through prayer, this enthusiasm grows. When you pray, the Holy Spirit prays in you. And the Spirit changes those praying through their prayers. This applies not only to this petition but to all petitions and supplications in prayer. The function of prayer is not to influence God, but to change the attitude of the person praying.

AND LET US NOT FALL INTO TEMPTATION

Let us not fall into temptation is a new and far more accurate translation than "Lead us not into temptation." It is Your guidance that helps us out of dangerous situations that we get ourselves lost in. Temptations are situations in life that threaten to bring us down like slipping on ice. We fall because we have no firm footing; we are not stable in ourselves.

Your name as Father is also decisive in this request. Jesus Christ taught us to recognize You, Unfathomable Mystery, our Great You, as our Father. Therefore, we also know who we ourselves are—Your children. This awareness is enough to steady our step. You don't even have to "intervene." The fact that we are aware of the dignity of being children of God allows us to stand upright. Strengthen me in this awareness when temptation threatens it. Amen.

Temptation is something that I usually experience as pressure from outside of me that is met by my inner urge to conform. I don't want to cause a stir, I don't want to be seen as a loner, even if that means lowering my moral standards a little. In doing so, however, I am giving into group conformity that can quickly turn into peer pressure. This is then met by my own willingness to make things easy for myself. I tell myself, "Everyone else does it, so why shouldn't I?" Now my standards have disappeared altogether, or to put it more accurately, public opinion has now become my standard.

Ethics, however, are anchored in human dignity and do not bow to external pressure. Ethics have their own collective voice and can contradict public opinion. Give me self-confidence and courage to do this, even when corruption becomes so widespread that it is hardly recognizable as such. Amen.

Temptation, if we give in to it, always leads to corruption—not always to bribery or manipulation, but something is always broken in the process. That is the original meaning of the word "corruption," from the Latin *rumpere*—"to break" and from *corrumpere*—"to undermine, to hurt, to destroy."

Temptation always threatens to shatter human dignity in one form or another. I feel that something is being suggested to me, that something is tempting and attracting me, which is beneath my dignity because I can call You "Father." The dignity of all other people is also at risk because we belong together as sisters and brothers.

If one becomes weak, all are weakened. But if one remains strong, even despite temptation, then that one strengthens all. This is not just about us humans either. All things and living creatures, because they belong to God's household, have their own inviolable dignity. Grant me reverence for this dignity of all living beings! Amen.

Temptation in all its forms ultimately puts our reverence to the test. It is always about reverence for You, O Great Mystery, for You are honored by our reverent fear of the dignity of Your presence in everything that exists. We become more aware of the dignity of our creaturely counterparts as we become more clearly aware of our own dignity as Your children; that is, as often as we consciously call You "Father."

To see the world in the light of Your fatherly love also means to form an image of Your worldwide household in its fullness of joy and peace. Only in contrast to this image of a perfect world do we become aware of how distorted a world is that knows no reverence. Not questioning this distorted world is the beginning of all temptation. Give me reverence and the courage to question all irreverence. Amen.

EVERY MOMENT CAN BECOME AN EXPERIENCE OF EASTER!

Brigitte: Can a good God lead us into temptation at all?

David: No. Not at all. The New Testament states explicitly, "God cannot be tempted by evil and he himself tempts no one" (James 1:13).

Brigitte: So why do we pray "Lead us not into temptation" in most churches when there is a better translation?

David: The new translation is better because it avoids the misunderstanding that God is testing us by "leading us into temptation." In Spanish, this request has always been translated in this sense (*No nos dejes caer en tentación*). In the official English and German versions, however, we still use the version "and lead us not into temptation," or *und führe uns nicht in Versuchung*. This is closer to the literal meaning of the original biblical text.

Brigitte: So where does the new translation come from?

David: In both Matthew and Luke we find the crucial phrase *mē eisenenkēis hēmas*. This is translated in its literal sense into Latin as *ne nos inducas*—"do not lead us into."

However, in order to be translated correctly, our passage in the Lord's Prayer must be consistent with the rest of Jesus's teachings.

Brigitte: Jesus teaches us to trust in God as a loving Father. How could a loving God tempt us deceitfully with traps?

David: Translating a sentence correctly does not necessarily mean translating it literally, but rather as it is intended. This failed a long time ago when the original Greek text was translated into the official Latin version. The new version "let us not fall into temptation" is actually a better translation of the original Greek text, because it is more accurate in meaning. That is why I even assume that the Latin version will soon be officially changed. After all, translations in all other languages are supposed to be based on it. The need for a new formulation becomes clear from the relationship between this request and the word "Father." The theme of forgiveness also shows that the word "Father" makes the request more understandable. The forgiveness of the loving Father is the archetype and active force behind our own forgiveness. Incidentally, all the petitions in the Lord's Prayer are connected to the word "Father" as if by threads on a loom.

Brigitte: The Father does not lead us not into temptation but leads us in temptation itself and through it.

David: And those who understand God as a loving Father, are strengthened by this trust in all temptations. The opposite is already shown in the story of the fall, which is precisely about people's mistrust of God. The actual temptation of Adam and Eve is directed against their childlike trust in God, who warned them as their Father. The tempter, the serpent, presents the warning as a tyrannical prohibition and thus God as a deceiver, "You will not die; for God knows that when you eat of it your eyes will be opened, and you will be like God" (Gen 3:4b–5).

Our first parents, who represent all of God's children, not only seriously damage their relationship with the Father through their mistrust, but they also become unfaithful to their understanding of themselves as children of God. There is a parallel between the biblical myth of Adam and Eve and our daily experience of temptation. In both cases, it is about remaining faithful not only to God, but also to oneself, despite the pressure in the opposite direction. In biblical imagery, this pressure is exerted by the serpent—the fearsome animal. Fear—often from peer pressure—is also what exerts the pressure in our temptations. That is why we call the transgression of our biblical first parents "original sin," not because it is the first sin, but because it shows what every sin is at its deepest core, namely, a relationship damaged due to fear.

Brigitte: When we give in to temptations in everyday life and don't stick to a diet, for example, it's not really damaging a relationship, it's just giving in, right?

David: Not being disciplined is first and foremost damaging the relationship with yourself. You're being unfaithful to yourself, perhaps only in a small way at first. But there are of course shades and variations here, as in all areas of human coexistence. Imagine, for example, that you are not sufficiently disciplined to resist the social pressure to drink an extra glass of wine before driving home. And then you have a serious accident in which someone might even die. Or a competitor of the company you work for wants to "buy" a trade secret from you, just at a time when you urgently need the money to pay for vital care that your elderly, sick mother needs. I can only hope not to fall into such a temptation myself.

Brigitte: This example takes us deep into the realm of far-reaching corruption.

David: The pressure of corruption can become so strong that the basic ethical principles in a community are completely lost—even for the next generation, because the previous has become a bad role model!

Brigitte: And yet it is possible to stand up against corruption, even as an individual.

David: Where should this attitude begin if not with disciplined resistance to even small temptations? Often, it is precisely the commitment to the community that requires us to act as individuals. The Lord's Prayer is a communal prayer, but it also gives us strength as individuals to act in accordance with our dignity as children of God.

Brigitte: What does this dignity mean to you?

David: The awareness of my dignity rests, so to speak, on two pillars: I know that as a human being I belong to all people, and I am aware of the responsibility to act independently in accordance with my ethical convictions. As I see it, this awareness of our dignity is inherent to every human being from the very beginning. But like so many things in life, it must develop step by step. After all, we only develop our innate ability to speak through our dialogical relationships. The same applies to our awareness of our human dignity. For this to happen, society needs to give us two things: unconditional acceptance and the right to self-determination—or to put it another way: belonging and independence. However, belonging and independence are always difficult to combine. Yet it is already possible in everyday situations, for example, when we listen with an open heart to a complete stranger on the bus. Being there for one another is the greatest gift we can give one another.

Brigitte: Unfortunately, not everyone experiences this kind of attention.

David: We can always be aware of one important truth: life itself gives us the two experiences we need to experience our human dignity. First, that we belong to life as a whole, and that the whole belongs to us.

Brigitte: People experience belonging to the whole in very different ways, some through pets, others through caring for plants or hiking in nature.

David: That is where the second experience comes in—that life holds us and carries us and embraces us, just as we are and no matter how damaged we may be. This fact can awaken in every person an awareness of their dignity and fill us with reverence for life and for each other.

Brigitte: However, our society is also very much permeated by a lack of reverence for one another.

David: Perhaps we should first ask what we actually mean by reverence.

Brigitte: The first thing that comes to mind is reverence or respect for life.

David: That seems like a very good approach to me. The word "reverence" is a stumbling block because it suggests a fearful awe, which implies a contradiction. Reverence for life is exactly the opposite of fear, namely, trust in life.

Brigitte: We sense a shyness in the face of the greatness of the whole, which feels like a kind of fear.

David: Hence the reference to "fear." The word "reverence" comes from the Latin word *verore*, which can mean both to respect or fear. The prefix "re-" suggests standing before the venerability of the whole in all its greatness.

Brigitte: In its greatness, yes, but also especially in its unfathomable depth.

David: Yes, the Great Mystery at the heart of the universe is unfathomably deep.

Brigitte: But our society today is not open to that.

David: Almost all cultures throughout history were open to the Great Mystery. That gave them a dimension of breathing room that we no longer know.

Brigitte: A society that is closed in on itself in this sense—trapped in itself—is a complete anomaly. We have locked ourselves in a prison.

David: That is why C. S. Lewis says, "The gates of hell are locked from the inside."[31] The kingdom of God means exactly the opposite of the hell that we have made our society into.

Brigitte: That is why there is another horizontal thread in our loom for the Lord's Prayer that connects the two petitions for protection in temptation and for the coming of the kingdom of God. When praying, it helps to know the structure of the Lord's Prayer.

David: On one hand is the kingdom of God and the power of love, and on the other hand, the temptation of the love of power.

Brigitte: And in the kingdom of God everyone shares everything with each other, but the constant temptation is the selfish accumulation of goods, money, privileges, gratifications, more and more.

David: Excessive "more and more" is the hallmark of our society. In God's kingdom, "less is more."

Brigitte: It's about quality over quantity.

David: In the midst of a society that has fallen deeply into temptation, the kingdom of God demands that we stand up.

Brigitte: We are required to stand up against an almost overpowering society.

David: After all, that is what "following Christ" means. But this standing up and resisting ultimately leads to a resurrection for us too.

Brigitte: That is possible at any moment. In this sense, every moment can become an experience of Easter.

BUT DELIVER US FROM EVIL

Evil? I should first ask myself what I am calling evil before I utter such a serious word so lightly. What can it mean? If You, the original Source of being, are good, then where does evil come from? How could evil even exist if existence itself is a great good?

Everything that is, is good! Evil lacks being. When I am ill, I say in German, *Mir fehlt etwas*, which literally means, "I'm missing something"—health in this case. Similarly, evil is also a lack. But what is this missing something? It may sound too simplistic when I say that evil lacks the "Yes of love," but this lack is really the greatest danger. Where love is lacking, even a kiss can become evil, a breach of trust, a betrayal of a friend, murder. So let me take evil seriously, but without being afraid of it. Amen.

Evil is a privation, a lack. It comes upon us when something necessary is missing. But there can also be evil in too much, because even in too much there can be something missing—the right relationship to the whole. For example, growth is good, but unlimited growth on a limited planet is a kind of cancer. The whole earth is suffering from this today.

Yes, all evils caused by humans in our times can ultimately be traced back to the population explosion. How should a loving couple react to this? Their "blessing of children" becomes a disaster for humanity. Then why do so few adopt orphans instead of bringing children into the world themselves? What they call love lacks a view of the bigger picture. Even religious institutions suffer from this shortsightedness. Let me always live the "Yes" of love with a view of the bigger picture. Amen.

Evil. I probably misunderstand this word so often because I too quickly think of it as being related to myself. Yet the word "I" does not appear once in the Lord's Prayer! The first two words, "Our Father" are intended to make us aware that we are praying in connection with the worldwide community of all God's children. This prayer is about our bread, our trespasses, and the evil from which we ask You to deliver us.

Evil is never a private matter. Today we talk about systemic evil, about that limitless disaster that none of us directly causes intentionally, but for which we are all jointly responsible. It is not malice that brings it upon us, but thoughtlessness and a lack of compassion. I even hear people say things like "Factory farms are simply necessary for today's agriculture," or "Without the arms industry, the economy would grind to a halt." Wake us up! Make us compassionate. Amen.

Evil—Is there such a thing as evil in nature? Over the course of my long life, it has become increasingly clear to me that the terms "good" and "evil" in the sense of life-affirming and life-denying are not applicable to natural events. In the long term, nature is always life-affirming, even when it destroys life. However, we humans live not only in the realm of nature, but also in the realm of ethics. We know that "good" and "evil" have unquestionable validity in the area of interpersonal relationships. Here, and from experience, we know evil as something that contradicts our ethical consciousness.

"Do not do to others what you do not want done to yourself." This ethical principle is valid for all people and is formulated in one way or another as obligatory in all cultures. This so-called golden rule sums up what "life-affirming" means in the human community. Natural events, on the other hand, occur outside of ethical judgments. Ethics begins with us humans. Let me do justice to this aspect of our human dignity by acting ethically, including by actively helping fellow human beings who are affected by natural disasters. Amen.

Deliver us, first of all, from the passive expectation that You will intervene "from on high" to redeem us without us having to use the redeeming power that You have placed in our hearts. Let us also recognize what this power consists of. If evil were a counterforce to good—both on the same level—then we would have to fight it in order to defeat it. In reality, however, evil is the "not-yet-good."

If we keep this in mind, we will understand the power to overcome evil in a completely different way. The "not-yet-good" demands patience from us, guidance, care, and loving encouragement so that it can grow into the good. This is exactly what a mother gives to a child who is not yet mature. Thus, let me look at evil with a mother's eyes and redeem it with Your motherly love that wants to flow through me. Amen.

Deliver us also through the power of righteous anger that we feel in our hearts when we face evil. Anger rises up in us as soon as we encounter evil in concrete terms, whether it's the bureaucracy that denies children on refugee boats the right to dock, the children who rummage through garbage dumps for food (who I have met and seen with my own eyes!), the children sold in human trafficking, or the little bodies that are emaciated by work, disfigured by hunger, or torn to pieces by landmines.

Anger, as a spontaneous reaction to such images of evil, comes from You. Indignation can trigger our readiness to act and contribute to salvation. We can harness anger into giving us patience and tenacious determination. My anger must burn so hot that it melts away all the dross of hatred and impatience. Free me from indifference, but also from impatience. Let me not shrink from any effort. Amen.

Deliver us through Your redeeming love, which wants to flow through us and in so doing, delivers us from apathy and indifference. These negative terms immediately suggest the awareness that we are missing something. What is missing is ultimately love—our lived "Yes" to belonging.

This "Yes" means, "I am here for you." That needs to be said—not always with words, but always clearly and helpfully—because otherwise "something is missing," indeed, the most important thing. This is how evil arises. It is far more often the result of small omissions than of genuine malice.

Although it starts so small, it can have unforeseeable wide ripples, gaining strength and causing terrible destruction. But even the smallest act of attention continues to have a healing and redeeming effect. Make me aware of the small beginnings of both evil and of redemption. Amen.

Deliver us through Your power, which our prayer opens the floodgates for. The flood of Your redeeming power is always dammed up and ready to wash away all my unkindness as soon as I open myself to it. I ask for this openness. Not that my asking changes Your mind; my prayer changes me.

I look at our wounded world and instead of despairing, I trustfully allow Your healing love to flow into my life and thus also into the world. Healing is the most apt image for what "deliverance" or "redemption" mean. The power of evil tears apart the delicate fabric of loving relationships, but the power of love connects us with one another again.

The invocation "Our Father" alone, spoken in prayer, testifies to our familial bond and is a step toward its realization. Jesus Christ became our Deliverer by trusting in the power of love even unto death. Bless me too with this gift of redeeming trust. Amen.

EVIL AS THE NOT-YET-GOOD

Brigitte: I find it difficult to imagine that evil, which we encounter everywhere, and which threatens us, is nothing.

David: What threatens us is, of course, something and not nothing. But what makes it evil is not an additional something, but a deficiency, and in this sense it is "nothing."

Brigitte: Experiences of accidents, theft, burglary, terror, conscious and unconscious injuries, and all kinds of injustice are the things that seem threatening to me.

David: With the word "injustice" you actually sum up your whole list of evil. And the negative prefix "in-" contains the crucial thing, namely, a negation. Evil in all its forms lacks something, namely, justice in all its forms. But justice has to do with alignment. The image behind it is the angle measuring tool that a carpenter uses to set the beams in the right proportion to one another. If the pieces fit together perfectly, they are said to be "justified." In the same way, justice aligns our relationships with a view to the whole. Where this alignment is missing, the whole house can collapse.

Brigitte: If I understand you correctly, you mean that the evil in evil is only a lack or deficiency. For example, a lack of correct alignment makes my relationship with the other person "evil."

David: This insight is already present in the German word for evil, *böse*. The original root, *bōsi*, actually meant "inflated, swollen," similar to the English word "boast," so evil is like a soap bubble that bursts and becomes nothing when I touch it.

Brigitte: An inflated nothing, then.

David: What makes the self become an ego is also just a deficiency. The ego lacks the awareness of self, the awareness of belonging. The self connects us all with one another. There is only one self in which we all have a part. And all ethically just behavior is rooted in this connection, in contrast to the separation that makes behavior evil.

Brigitte: How do we then deal with evil when we encounter it?

David: My favorite image for this is that we don't look at evil with the eyes of an enemy, but with the eyes of a loving mother. She doesn't sugarcoat what is bad about the child's behavior, but her unconditionally loving attitude creates a space in which what is not yet good can grow into something that is.

Brigitte: Your observation clearly shows that evil can be either too little or too much of something.

David: Both too much and too little lack balance.

Brigitte: And how do we stay in balance?

David: By looking at the whole. The philosophical concept of the "nexus of the whole" (*Zusammenhang des Ganzen*) can refer to both relationship to the whole or the network of connections within the whole.

Brigitte: Today, this is about the global context. It is about the cooperation of all nations on earth. But what guarantees this cohesion for us?

David: The disintegration of our world comes from the fact that the view of the Great Mystery is no longer binding and authoritative for our society as a whole. It is only at home in religion, and today religion is often dismissed as folklore. In the language of the Our Father, one could say that we lack cohesion as children of God today because we have forgotten our common relationship with the Father. But we can all work against the separation and polarization and instead contribute something to healing the world. We just have to strive to find the right balance. In our private lives, we are always pushing for "more, more, more" like children blowing up their balloons until they burst. It is always about the right balance. One of my friends, an expert in economic issues, often amazes me. He shows that there is a grotesque disparity between income and voluntary social donations, and this applies to all sections of the population. The only exception is the very poorest. They may not be able to donate much, but they share more happily than anyone else.

Brigitte: In our society, time constraints often make us blind and deaf to everything that life wants to tell us.

David: There is a sonnet by Rilke that is so important to me that I have memorized it. I know it "by heart," as we say in English, and I do carry it in my heart.

We are the driving ones.
Ah, but the step of time:
think of it as a dream
in what forever remains.

All that is hurrying
soon will be over with;
only what lasts can bring
us to the truth.

Young men, don't put your trust
into the trials of flight,
into the hot and quick.

All things already rest:
darkness and morning light,
flower and book.[32]

How important it is to listen to what life wants to tell us, as our ancestors have always taught their children. Do you remember, for example, the fairy tale about *Frau Holle* or "Mother Hulda" from the Brothers Grimm? A young girl falls into a well, discovering another world where loaves of bread ask to be taken out of an oven and she does, apples ask to be picked from a tree and she does, then an old woman, Frau Holle, asks her to help around the house and she does. When she shakes the pillows, the feathers fall making it snow in the real world. The girl is rewarded with gold, but her younger stepsister who later comes to do the same, neglects the bread, apples, and housework so she is only rewarded with tar.

Brigitte: Of course, Goldmarie, the older sister, listens to life, and Pechmarie, the younger stepsister, is deaf to it. Goldmarie listens to the oven, the apple tree, and *Frau Holle*. Pechmarie, on the other hand, is as deaf as a stone to them all.

David: These are diametrically opposed attitudes toward life. What speaks from the oven and the apple tree is life itself in its form as culture and nature. And Frau Holle in the fairy tale comes from an ancient female earth goddess. She is a personification of the Great Mystery in the heart of nature, the "Our Mother." So we are not going too far from the Lord's Prayer here. Pechmarie misses the path of "us-thinking" that leads Goldmarie to her radiant happiness.

Brigitte: We often barely take the time for a mindful

conversation and therefore don't give others the opportunity to be seen or heard.

David: If we live the "Yes" to our connectedness, we overcome evil. In the innermost heart of nature, we encounter the Great Mystery that is also present in the human heart. Only the lived "Yes" of love can overcome the "No" of evil. This also means not being afraid of evil. That demands a lot from us, because evil is indeed terrifying. We should face it in all its seriousness and courageously confront the fear that evil incites in us. We must endure the fear, but that does not mean we must be afraid. Because God is, but evil is not.

Brigitte: The devil cannot be an equal opponent of God.

David: The evil mentioned in the petition, "Deliver us from evil" has very often been understood as the "evil one," the personification of the devil. We even find references to Satan, Beelzebub, or the devil in various books of the Old and New Testaments. All of these images are embodiments of evil. The book of Job, for example, tries to express this when it personifies the power of evil as Satan and calls him an "angel of God," an "angel" in the sense of "servant of God." The decisive point is that the Bible never presents "evil" as a comparable opposite pole to God, but always as subordinate, as an "angel" in the sense of a servant.

Brigitte: How then should we imagine this deliverance and liberation?

David: "The Way" is a very important keyword here. Even before Christians were called Christians, they were known as those who "belonged to the Way." This meant the way of redemption and deliverance. They also called Jesus not only the "Deliverer" or "Redeemer," but also the "Way"—the Way to Freedom, we could say. The goal is freedom. This word better expresses what is actually meant by deliverance, namely, liberation. Just setting out on the Way already has a liberating effect. However, steady progress leads us to ever greater freedom.

Brigitte: The word "Way" itself indicates that it is a life-long path of practice. The three virtues "faith, hope, and love" can be important signposts along the way.

David: Connection liberates. Faithful trust connects us with the Great Mystery. Hopeful willingness to become more authentic step by step connects us with our true selves. Our loving "Yes" to belonging connects us with all living beings. But sin tears these three bonds of connection apart. But we experience salvation—as both a gift and a task—in three forms of connection. Faith liberates our hearts through trust in God's absolute trustworthiness. Hope delivers us through openness to surprise at every step of the way. Finally, love heals us through the warmth of our hearts with which we receive God's "Yes" and actively pass it on. Ultimately, it is about "becoming real"—this phrase best sums up the essence of salvation. In the classic children's book by Margery Williams, *The Velveteen Rabbit*, the dolls and teddy bears talk at night about their greatest wish: to become real. "Does becoming real hurt?" they ask the old, experienced rocking horse. But he knows that someone who becomes real doesn't mind that it hurts.

Brigitte: You say that anger in the face of evil is a reaction that drives us to act. But how am I supposed to understand those Bible passages that say that God is angry with people?

David: Thinking that the Bible is a handbook dictated by God only entangles us in contradictions. It is not one book at all, but a collection of many books of very different kinds—myths, historiography, prayers, love songs, gospels, letters. Texts in which people have wrestled with the Great Mystery for thousands of years. Judeo-Christian tradition canonizes these writings as the Bible because it recognizes their innermost essence in them.

Brigitte: Ultimately, that makes these texts much more venerable than if we consider them to be God's inerrant instruction manual for a spiritual life.

David: When reading the biblical passages about God's wrath, we can therefore always rightly think of holy wrath. This allows us to admire the authors' longing for justice behind this "wrath of God," even if they often express their indignation all too vehemently.

Brigitte: You keep saying that evil is not something, but rather a lack of something essential. But how can a lack attain such overwhelming power?

David: Evil can grow from the smallest of beginnings over long periods of time, from generation to generation. Some areas of the tremendous power with which evil confronts us today may have needed thousands of years to gain the force they possess today. Our redemption begins with reflection and reconnection with the Great Mystery that connects us all. From this connection arises the power of good to heal our environment and our fellow human beings. In private life, this means that I must "fill up" my indebtedness with forgiveness, unforgiveness with pardon, discontent with joy. Discrimination is also ultimately due to a lack, the lack of empathy. This requires enlightenment and the education of the heart, but we can only impart this to a new generation through appropriate schooling. Redemption from evil demands our entire commitment, not only on a personal level, but especially on a social level. If we embrace those closest to us as well as those furthest from us with the same warmth of heart, this gives us an unimagined inner breadth and freedom. In this sense, we can all be mediators of the healing power of the Great Mystery, a power that flows through the entire cosmos. In this sense we are all priests and priestesses. The more I allow this healing, redeeming power to flow through me, the more it makes me whole.

Brigitte: If we allow this redeeming power to flow and pass it on, we become completely permeable to the Great Mystery.

David: A touching example comes to mind. At a time when ships were still the only way to travel between America and Europe, my mother was standing on the deck of the trans-atlantic ship, the SS Bremen, in New York Harbor. Down on the pier, she noticed the tearful farewell of a large Italian family who had entrusted a severely disabled young woman in a wheelchair to a group of fellow travelers. During the crossing, my mother took care of the young woman, named Teresa, who had great difficulty leaving her tiny and overheated cabin on the lowest deck. She learned that the family could only afford one ticket, and so her daughter had to travel to Lourdes alone, to pray for her healing. When they arrived in France, the group of pilgrims to whom Teresa had been entrusted disembarked with her in Le Havre. My mother stayed on board until Hamburg, but for a long time she could not forget the rock-solid hope with which the sick woman had prayed for healing at that place of grace. After many months, a letter came from Teresa; she had never reached Lourdes. There wasn't a word about the circumstances under which she had been left alone in a Paris hotel room. But even the poor stationary seemed to be radiant. The letter spoke nothing but overflowing gratitude for all the help and blessings that Teresa had received from countless helpful people. There was nothing but joy at being reunited with her family in the United States. The letter did not speak at all of forgiveness or healing, but it testified to redemption—deliverance—through love. And deliverance ultimately comes down to love.

AMEN

Amen. With this one word I summarize once again what every single sentence in the Lord's Prayer is trying to express, namely, my trust in Your limitless trustworthiness. As "Our Father," You are the Archetype of Unshakable "Firmness." Firmness is the root meaning of the Hebrew word "Amen." From this root in Hebrew comes Your mystical name "Truth" as well as the word for "believe." Such a belief means much more than believing certain sentences to be true—it expresses a reliance, a reliance on Your dependability. There is no other way to experience this than trust, because I cannot deduce Your reliability from logical conclusions alone.

But I can experience Your reliability irrefutably as Your presence in my own vitality, O Great Mystery of Life. Every breath proves to me that I am reliably supported by a Life Force that I cannot understand. Life itself, in all its development, keeps saying "Yes!" to all its forms in their coming into being and passing away. From this "Yes" of all that exists, I can hear a cosmic "Amen" as an answer to Your "Yes" to being. I can also keep repeating this "Yes" with my whole being. Amen.

Amen is not only something we should think of at the end, but also within the Lord's Prayer, because "Amen" expresses our agreement and participation. Therefore, we should hear it resonating in every single petition. "Amen" is the mutual "Yes" of God and people. The whole prayer is characterized by reciprocity. Even the first petition, that we may prove ourselves worthy of Your name, presupposes reciprocity between You as Father and us as Your children. The coming of Your kingdom—the reign of God—is Your gift, but at the same time it is also our task. And Your will will only be done on earth when we do it. Even our daily bread only becomes a true gift when we receive it with gratitude. The request for forgiveness, "as we forgive," expresses the reciprocity that is woven into the "Amen" through its very formulation. You protect us from temptation by giving us the strength to prove ourselves, and You deliver us from evil by giving us the strength to break free from evil. You honor me so greatly through reciprocity! Let me honor You too. Amen.

Amen is not just the liturgical conclusion after a prayer, but rather a promise to actively commit ourselves to what we are praying for. "Amen" means, "So be it!"—the beginning of my own actions. But is it really my own actions? It is Your breath of life, Father, that fuels my prayers and actions. What burns in every petition of the Our Father is Your Holy Spirit. In the Christian tradition, seven spiritual gifts are attributed to the Holy Spirit. These can also be found in the Our Father: I can only sanctify and praise Your name in a spirit of (1) reverence. Only in a spirit of (2) understanding can I contribute to Your kingdom coming, because standing up for it and understanding it presuppose one another. In order to do Your will, I must know it, and only Your spirit of (3) knowledge can teach me that. (4) Wisdom—*sapientia*—in its original meaning is the gift of discernment. Only in the spirit of wisdom can I therefore distinguish between poisonous food and the bread for which I pray. Mutual forgiveness of sins is only possible in the spirit of (5) piety, because piety really means a sense of the whole, a sense of family, a sense of our brother- and sisterhood as your children. Through the gift of Your (6) counsel Your Holy Spirit protects us from temptation and redeems us through Your (7) fortitude. In Your Holy Spirit, I breathe and pray, Amen.

Amen connects me, whenever I say it in prayer, with all my sisters and brothers in the "Amen traditions," because Jews, Christians, and Muslims all conclude and confirm their prayers with "Amen." How fitting that one word connects the three traditions, because the word is in the center of all three. In Buddhism, however, silence is central, which is why the foundational trust is expressed not in a word but in silence. And for the understanding-through-action that characterizes Hindu spirituality, "Amen" also consists in doing—in trusting, loving action.

What "Amen" wants to express is radical trust in the deepest trustworthiness of being. Trust is the basic attitude of every successful human life, completely independent of this or that religious tradition. That is why I consciously connect myself with all Your children in this world when I solemnly conclude my personal reflections on this prayer to our common Father with "Amen."

THE LORD'S PRAYER HAS SIGNIFICANCE BEYOND THE CHRISTIAN TRADITION

David: The Life Force not only works in creation, but also in ourselves. After all, we don't start breathing at will and we don't stop at will either. What we experience is the Incomprehensible Mystery of the Life in which we live and which lives in us. From the first to the last breath, Life lives in us. Rilke speaks of the "midst of the Ever, in which you breathe and surmise."[33] And C. S. Lewis says, "There is no way out of the center save into the Bent Will which casts itself into the Nowhere."[34] The Life Force is an undeniable experience for us and at the same time an unfathomable mystery. Whether we want to call it "God" or not is up to us. It is important that we understand that this is not just about the right perspective, but also about the right attitude—not only our vision and thinking are challenged, but also our will. That is why C. S. Lewis speaks of the "Bent Will which casts itself into the Nowhere." By this he means our refusal to rely on the Great Mystery.

Brigitte: Well, relying on ourselves is always a challenge.

David: What we are then approaching is, in this case, a great adventure. "Amen," understood in its full sense, means embarking on the adventure of encountering the Great Mystery. One image for this is, "letting myself fall into the hands of the Lord."[35]

But it's not just about letting go. Each of the seven petitions of the Lord's Prayer is only fulfilled through a give-and-take between God and humans. We are invited to a relationship with God that does not diminish us and make us small, but rather elevates us to become coworkers with God. The interaction between God and humans is often expressed in the image of the cosmic dance. And the poet W. B. Yeats asks the question, "How can we know the dancer from the dance?"[36]

Brigitte: The great dance is a very beautiful image for the whole.

David: Yes, for the whole. But if I only look at parts, then I might see limping, staggering, jostling, and slipping. "Dancing" seems to be almost euphemistic as an image for the whole. That's also comforting, though, because even the not-yet-good is part of the whole. Our freedom consists in finding very personal dance moves to respond to the music of life.

Brigitte: No matter how difficult it gets, we can still say, in the words of Holocaust survivor and author Victor Frankl, "Yes to Life."[37] That's part of dancing too!

David: We are not dancing marionettes, but free dancers. Only by overcoming difficulties do we find the full meaning of our existence.

Brigitte: Listening obediently to the music of life and freely creating our own dance moves in response to it—that's what the great dance is all about.

David: I like the way you juxtapose obedience and freedom. The image implies that obedience does not mean slavishly following orders, but free, loving listening.

Brigitte: Why do you mention the seven gifts of the Holy Spirit in your meditation?

David: For me personally, it is helpful to not only open my heart in a general way to the enthusiasm of the Holy Spirit, but also to specifically name the individual spiritual gifts such as reverence, wisdom, or fortitude. This makes my prayers for the Holy Spirit much more vivid. Some gifts, such as understanding and knowledge, are not so easy to distinguish between at first. That is why I tried to assign the individual spiritual gifts to the various Lord's Prayer petitions. For most of the gifts, it was not difficult for me to assign them to a petition. It's easy to see that I need counsel in temptation and fortitude for deliverance from evil. I found it more difficult to assign corresponding gifts to the two petitions for the coming of the kingdom of God and for the fulfillment of

FATHER

NAME
Fear of God/Reverence

KINGDOM
Understanding

WILL
Knowledge

REDEMPTION
Fortitude

PROTECTION
Counsel

FORGIVENESS
Piety

BREAD
Wisdom

God's will. However, it soon became clear to me that we need knowledge to recognize God's will. And the kingdom of God can only come if we place ourselves in it. Understanding is a type of insight that we can only gain from within, because such "*in*sight" requires "being inside." For example, you can know everything about swimming, but to really know how to swim you have to get wet. And to understand the kingdom of God you have to be working to bring it about.

Of course, each person praying can assign the spiritual gifts differently, depending on their own associations, as they see fit. For example, I know someone who makes a reference to the cross in every request. The cross as a sign of victory hallows God's name. The kingdom of God comes in the sign of the cross. We ask that God's will be done, even if it thwarts our will. There is already a time-honored connection between the cross and daily bread through meditation in the traditional translation of the Bible verse Jeremiah 11:19 (Douay-Rheims version): "Let us put wood"—the wood of the cross—"on his bread, and cut him off from the land of the living." The cross is the symbol of the forgiveness of sins, the protective shield in temptation, and the key to salvation. Of course, everyone can come up with such personal enrichments to the Lord's Prayer themselves.

Brigitte: Looking back, I am amazed that the Lord's Prayer, the main prayer of Christianity, is formulated in such a way that we can actually make it our own, regardless of our particular religious tradition.

David: I've never thought of it in those terms, but I think that's right. The Lord's Prayer does contain some distinctly Christian words such as calling God "Father," "kingdom of God," and "deliver," but it removes any exclusivity from these terms, making them accessible to everyone.

Brigitte: That's right, everyone can understand what is meant by it.

David: Properly understood, "kingdom of God" should also make sense for everyone—as the peaceful world that all people long for. We are not the only ones longing for and hoping for our solidarity as free-willed people in a world of peace. One could even understand the whole of human history as a difficult struggle to practically realize the values of a peaceful world through mutual trust. We can only realize these values through the greatest possible common effort, both in public and in private life.

Brigitte: That is why Buddhist activist Thích Nhất Hạnh says in his lecture on prayer, "The Lord's Prayer is a prayer of action."[38]

David: An action that arises from our gaze on God as Father. The Lord's Prayer is therefore a contemplative prayer in the sense that contemplation involves the realization through loving action of the ideal image we have seen.

Brigitte: But "contemplative" and "active" are generally understood as opposites.

David: Yes, but there is a mistake behind that. Contemplation comes from the Latin word *contemplatio*, which means looking to heaven as a guide for our earthly actions. That is what the Lord's Prayer means by "on earth as it is in heaven." Whenever we pray the Lord's Prayer, we open the eyes of our hearts anew and see how God's name, God's kingdom, and God's will want to become our standard here and now. We even allow ourselves to shape our world according to this standard. In this sense, it is the contemplative prayer par excellence.

Brigitte: When praying the Lord's Prayer together, we often add, "For thine is the kingdom, and the power, and the glory."

David: This is a very old addition to the Lord's Prayer that summarizes its structure again. In the descending requests (name→will→kingdom), everything is directed toward the KINGDOM of God, the ascending series (forgiveness→protection→deliverance) culminates in the GLORY of God, which becomes visible in creation liberated to full vitality. The realization of the kingdom and liberation springs from the POWER that our daily bread gives us. Understood in this way, "bread" reveals the ultimate depth of the meaning of the Eucharist, the "Body of Christ."

Brigitte: All these longitudinal and transverse connections seem like the warp and woof, the vertical and horizontal weaving, on a large loom of prayer.

David: That is a beautiful image. The final "Amen" then ties up everything that we weave in prayer in a great and final loving "Yes, Father!"

THANKS

"Respect for life" is the path I have followed since my early youth, following in the footsteps of Albert Schweitzer. I would like to thank from the bottom of my heart the many people who have been and are a light for me on this path.

In my everyday professional life, my encounter with Brother David Steindl-Rast, OSB, changed my perspective on health and illness and, from 2007 onward, initiated training courses that have made me more alive. The spirit of the European Monastery Gut Aich in St. Gilgen and the Kardinal König House in Vienna became the foundations of the volunteer service that I built upon. Since then, countless people have become important companions to me or have ignited sparks in me; I am grateful for the encounters with Father Johannes Pausch, OSB, Brother Thomas Hessler, OSB, Susanne Gross, Hans Fuchs, Silvia Fuchs-Egger, Mirjam Luthe, and Kristina Proleta as well as for encounters with Christian Marte, JS, Sister Karin Weiler, CS, Silvia Langthaler, Desideria Trappl, and Ilse Reisinger.

I owe the joy and enthusiasm of getting to the bottom of my heart's longing to Brother David Steindl-Rast. His life exemplifies what Rainer Maria Rilke speaks of in his *Letters to a Young Poet*: "Do you remember how this life, from childhood, longed for something great?" Our community began with the founding of the Grateful Living Network in Europe in 2012. From the very beginning, our joint work has been characterized by vitality, light-heartedness, and humor, by mutual trust in our actions and by enthusiasm for our common concerns. This has found expression, for example, in film projects such as the documentary film *Erfülltes Leben: Wenn die Schale überfließt* (A fulfilled life: When the bowl overflows) made with Hans Fuchs, and in several book projects which I collaborated on.

The fact that Brother David Steindl-Rast has now invited me to a short conversation about his reflections on the Lord's Prayer is a special gift for which I am sincerely grateful. I entered into the dialogues with a sense of great joy, responsibility, and courage, and I was able to experience cowriting as a process of finding words from the heart. I would also like to thank my friends and family from the bottom of my heart for their understanding that a lot of time is necessary for accompanying people on their journey and carrying out projects. I feel grateful to all the people who care for others in their families, circles of friends, and neighbors, in their jobs or in their volunteer work, and I say a heartfelt thank you to you all.

Brigitte Kwizda-Gredler

To these words of thanks from my conversation partner, I would like to add my thanks for her invaluable help. It is clear from the text itself how much her ingenuity has enriched our conversations. We both owe thanks to Father Wolfgang Kimmel and Klaus Semsroth for carefully reading our draft texts and for valuable suggestions. Tyrolia Publishing and publishing director Gottfried Kompatscher and our editor Klaus Gasperi also deserve great thanks. But as soon as I begin to think gratefully about how many people have helped directly or indirectly with this book, I come across an incalculable network that ultimately spans the entire world. Many of them may never hear of the Lord's Prayer and yet we are all children of the Great Mystery and brothers and sisters to one another; for that, I am most grateful.

Brother David Steindl-Rast, OSB
Easter 2022, Güelta de Areco, Azcuénaga, Argentina

NOTES

1. This is a particularly difficult paragraph to translate as it relies on German palindromes. The first pairing is *Tor/rot* (gate/red), the second is *Gras/Sarg* (grass/coffin), and the "rather profound" third one is *Leben/Nebel* (life/fog). The phrase "repentance = purgatory" is *Reue = Fegefeur* and the imperative to "lazy students" is the harsher *Lese, Esel!* (Read, donkey!). *Reizend lügt güldene Zeir* is similar to the English expression "All that glitters is not gold," and literally means "Golden ornament charmingly deceives."

2. From the poem "Talismane, Amulete, Abraxas, Inschriften und Siegel," as translated in Stokes, *The Book of Lieder.*

3. Stokes, *Book of Lieder.*

4. From the poem "Der Schutzengel." Translation from Rilke, *The Book of Images.*

5. *No nos dejes caer en tentación* and *Ne nous laisse pas entrer en tentation*, respectively.

6. From Shakespeare, *Othello.*

7. *Die Welt ist groß, klein ist der Verstand.*

8. The German original has *Kauf beim Spar / Spar beim kauf*, a slogan for the supermarket chain SPAR, meaning "Shop at Spar, Save when you shop."

9. From the poem "Dir ist mein Beten keine Blasphemie" as translated in Rilke's *Book of Hours.*

10. From "Sonnets to Orpheus," II, 14. As translated in Rilke, *Ahead of All Parting.*

11. From the poem "Immer wieder." As translated in Rilke's *Book of Hours.*

12. Original translation of the poem "Es wandelt, was wir schauen." From *Gedichte.*

13. As translated in Münsterberg, *A Harvest of German Verse.*

14. As translated in Rilke, "Abend in Skåne."

15. Original translation.

16. From "Sonnets to Orpheus," II,16. As translated in Rilke, *Ahead of All Parting.*

17. From Rilke's "Du Dunkelheit, aus der ich stamme." As translated in Rilke's *Book of Hours.*

18. This and the next lines are from "Es tauchten tausend Theologen" by Rilke. Original translation.

19. Translation from Barrows and Macy, *A Year with Rilke.*

20. As translated in Bly, *The Kabir Book.*

21. *Was hier wir sind, kann dort ein Gott ergänzen.* Attributed to the German poet Friedrich Hölderlin.

22. From Rilke's poem "Wer seines Lebens viele Widersinne." As translated in Rilke, Rilke's *Book of Hours.*

23. "Hier liegt vor deiner Majestät" is a hymn by Michael Haydn (1737–1806), to be sung during the *Kyrie,* emphasizing humanity's role at the bottom of the divine power hierarchy.

24. As translated in Teilhard de Chardin, *Toward the Future.*

25. From "Sonnets to Orpheus," I, 12. As translated in Rilke, *Ahead of All Parting.*

26. Original translation.

27. Translation from Rilke, *Ahead of All Parting.*

28. "Sonnets to Orpheus," II, 2. As translated in Rilke, *Ahead of All Parting.*

29. From an exposition on Psalm 148. As translated in Augustine, *Expositions on the Psalms.*

30. From *Die unsichtbare Loge.* As translated in Richter, *The Invisible Lodge.*

31. Lewis, *The Great Divorce.*

32. "Sonnets to Orpheus," I, 22. As translated in Rilke, *Ahead of All Parting.*

33. From "Elegy to Marina Tsvetayeva-Efron." As translated in Rilke.

34. Lewis, *Perelandra.*

35. See 2 Sam 24:14, for example.

36. From "Among School Children."

37. See Frankl, *Yes to Life.*

38. Thích, "Dharma Talk."

REFERENCES

Augustine. *Expositions on the Psalms*. Translated by A. Cleveland Coxe. Nicene and Post-Nicene Fathers, First Series 8. Edinburgh: T&T Clark, 1886.

Barrows, Anita, and Joanna Macy. *A Year with Rilke: Daily Readings from the Best of Rainer Maria Rilke*. New York: HarperOne, 2009.

Bly, Robert, ed. *The Kabir Book: Forty-Four of the Ecstatic Poems of Kabir*. Translated by Robert Bly. Boston: Beacon Press, 1993.

Frankl, Viktor E. *Yes to Life: In Spite of Everything*. Translated by Joelle Young. Boston: Beacon Press, 2020.

Hạnh, Thích Nhât. "The Practice of Prayer." *The Mindfulness Bell* 17 (1996): 1–14.

Lewis, C. S. *The Great Divorce*. Revised ed. San Francisco: HarperOne, 2001.

———. *Perelandra*. Hudson River Editions. New York: Macmillan, 1990.

Münsterberg, Margarete, ed. *A Harvest of German Verse*. Translated by Margarete Münsterberg. New York: D. Appleton, 1916.

Richter, Jean Paul. *The Invisible Lodge*. Translated by Charles T. Brooks. New York: United States Book Company, 1883.

Rilke, Rainer Maria. "Abend in Skåne." Translated by Owen Lucas. *Plume* 74 (September 2017).

———. *Ahead of All Parting: The Selected Poetry and Prose of Rainer Maria Rilke*. Translated by Stephen Mitchell. First ed. New York: Modern Library, 1995.

———. *The Book of Images*. Revised bilingual ed. Translated by Edward Snow. New York: North Point Press, 1994.

———. *Rilke's Book of Hours: Love Poems to God*. Translated by Anita Barrows and Joanna Macy. Reprint, New York: Riverhead Books, 2005.

Stokes, Richard, ed. *The Book of Lieder: The Original Texts of Over 1000 Songs*. Translated by Richard Stokes. London: Faber and Faber, 2005.

Teilhard de Chardin, Pierre. *Toward the Future*. Translated by René Hague. San Diego: Harcourt, 2002. http://archive.org/details/TowardTheFuture.